Celestial ✵ Psychology®

A Workbook of

Chakras, Psychological Theory

&

Conscious Evolution

To My Cousin
Virginia –
My BFF + Life's Sojourner Buddy!

Thank you for all
Your Support +
Belief in me
All → this Lifetime!

— Celeste ♡

Celestial ✹ Psychology®

A Workbook of
Chakras, Psychological Theory
&
Conscious Evolution

Celeste Emelia Mattingly, LCSW

Editing, Layout and Design by Linda Moore

Adam Kadmon Publishing

adamkadmonpublishing.com

Published by
Adam Kadmon Publishing
P.O. Box 33039
West Hartford, Connecticut 06133
USA

Celestial Psychology®: A Workbook of Chakras, Psychological Theory & Conscious Evolution
Copyright © 2012 by Celeste Emelia Mattingly, LCSW

Contributor Dory Dzinski may be contacted via dorydzinski.com.

The information in this book is educational and is not intended to replace any form of medical treatment or 12-Step recovery program. The author, contributors, and publisher are in no way liable or responsible for any misuse of this material, either directly or indirectly.

Edit, layout, design, and Celestial Psychology® logo by
Linda Moore, Cambridge Project Resources
linda@cambridgeprojectsresources.com

Cover design by Monty Jorgensen, Chrysalis Creative Group
chrysaliscreativegroup.com

Celestial Psychology® mandala by Jo Thomas Blaine

Ambika Wauters, author, granted permission to print her list of chakra properties and the archetypal paragraphs from: *The Book of Chakras: Discover the Hidden Forces Within You.* (2002)

Printed in the United States of America.
Includes full-color illustrations, bibliographical references and glossary

ISBN-13: 978-0-9859819-1-4
celestialpsychology.com
celestemattinglylcsw.com

Celestial Psychology® is a registered trademark of Celeste Mattingly US Patent and Trademark Office. First use May 2008, Official August 2010 SN: 77479914.

This workbook is dedicated
to the human race.

Contents

Preface

Are you worrying more and wondering, what's going on in this crazy world of ours? Are you freaked out by how fast time is flying by? Are you finding yourself overwhelmed by pathos or tragedy or isolation? Have you been having physiological symptoms that medical doctors can't explain? Perhaps you have experienced a weird sensation of the ground falling beneath you or you sometimes think you hear the sounds of our mother earth, Gaia, groaning under the weighty fallout of our disrespect. Do you find yourself vacillating between profound despair and all-knowing elation, making you wonder if something in you needs to be fixed, perhaps with clinical intervention or bi-polar medication? Are you experiencing a sense of urgency to "wake-up!" as if your existence to this point has been some sort of dream?

If you answered yes to any of the above, this workbook is for you. Perhaps you are interested in chakras or psychological theory or conscious evolution and wondering how these topics could possibly interconnect has peaked your interest. If so, you already know this workbook is for you. Whether you are a professional in the field or an individual *Work*ing* to improve your QOL, and inevitably elevating the

*See WORK and HOLY WORK OF CP in Glossary.

collective, this workbook is for you.

The body of work introduced in these pages was *propelled into existence* by a sense of urgency that I originally understood to be my personal need to understand questions like the ones above. This sense of urgency which began several decades ago, has grown from a vague and inexplicable murmur to an ever-increasing and profoundly compelling force that continues to push me beyond my comfort zones.

The need to figure out what's going on in our crazy world, has been a gift of desperation that began when I was a small child growing up in a painfully dysfunctional family. By the time I was in high school, metaphysics and the world's religions brought comfort and peaked my interest—no doubt an abreaction to the religiosity of Catholic dogma and education. I became a seeker of knowledge looking to expand my comprehension of life and *being*. In college, I became an avid experimenter in all sorts of consciousness-raising activities. (Yes, go ahead and use your imagination. Someday I'll reveal all the juicy details…maybe…) I was introduced to energy balancing and the chakra system in the early 1970s.

For the past thirteen years, I have worked with hundreds of clients as a holistically-oriented, *licensed* psychotherapist. I studied numerous philosophies and healing modalities, and became a facilitator of *The Reconnection*® in 2008. That was the year I realized I had to take my work as a psychotherapist to a new level.

Initially, I trademarked the name *Celestial Psychology*® and desired only to articulate what makes my work as a psychotherapist different from approaches offered by other providers. However, while trying to do that, this sense of urgency to find meaning and make sense of my work, my own life, and life in general continues to gain momentum.

While working on these chapters, waves of aha moments, profound synchronicity, increased perseverance, and tingling scalp sensations caused me to declare, "This is different, this *Work* is working me!" Every bit of knowledge I gained, anecdotal evidence I found, and theoretical approach I researched, along with every new and old consciousness-raising experience I have while doing my own *Work* strengthens my conviction that something radical is happening to me, to the species and to our planet.

Thankfully, I have learned this strange compelling sense of urgency that has been pushing me beyond my comfort zone is in fact being called by scientists, scholars, metaphysicians, and futurists the evolutionary impulse. This exciting realization lead to the inevitable creation of something with more far-reaching effects than birthing a new psychological theory. It is the birth of a new, major wave of psychology—Conscious Evolutionary Psychology—and Celestial Psychology is its primary defining theoretical framework.

In the pages ahead, I will detail this new wave of psychology, inspired by authors and great thinkers like Ken Wilber, Andrew Cohen, Barbara Marx Hubbard, Carter Phipps, and others to whom I am eternally grateful. Their wisdom and ideas have enriched me and increased my consciousness in ways I never imagined. Thanks to them, I now have a much deeper understanding of the workings of the mind, spirit, ego and essence. On numerous occasions, I was overcome with joy, awe, and gratitude while working on this project. In particular when I read the following quote from Ken Wilber's *Integral Psychology*, I was overwhelmed with the synchronicity of my own inspirations. On page 194 Wilber states:

> "Kosmic evolution is now producing theories and performances of its own integral embrace...connect[ing] the previously unconnected, and pull[ing] together the fragments of a world too weary to endure."
> —**Ken Wilber**

Over the last few years during the on-going process of writing this theory, I also stumbled upon a fascinating correlation between the chakra system, the historical development of psychological theory and the evolution of mankind. I began presenting this in my *7 Weeks to Spiritual Empowerment* class. The material evolved into a workshop that I presented with my colleague Dory Dzinski, LPC for clinicians as well as laypersons. The workshop was authorized by the National Association of Social Worker's Connecticut Chapter in order for 7.5

Continuing Education Credits (CECs) to be awarded to Licensed Clinical Social Workers (LCSWs), Licensed Marriage and Family Therapists (LMFTs), and Licensed Professional Counselors (LPCs). This correlation alone has the capacity to promote profound and lasting change. Combined with the revolutionary concepts for healing, the Holy Work exercises for consciousness-raising and the arousal of the evolutionary impulse, I believe the pages of this workbook will elevate your consciousness the way writing it has elevated mine.

> Something with more far-reaching effects than birthing a new psychological theory *is* taking place: it is the birth of a new, major wave of psychology—Conscious Evolutionary Psychology—and Celestial Psychology is its primary defining theoretical framework.

Acknowledgments

I must start with a special mention to everyone, whether I know you personally or not, who is in recovery from substance abuse, mental illness, or a life-threatening physical illness. Thank you for showing me beyond the shadow of a doubt that those who have been to hell and back again bring a little piece of heaven to Earth. I am eternally grateful to all the students, colleagues, and clients who helped to shape this workbook.

Special thanks to my colleague Dory Dzinski, LPC for her contributions to this project. Her knowledge of the chakra system is integrated throughout the text and her *Guided Visualizations* are sure to benefit all who take the time to utilize and enjoy them.

I also acknowledge all the authors in the bibliography who have influenced me over the years. They don't know it, but many of them have become my imaginary friends! LOL! The textbook written by Prochaska and Norcross began my wheels spinning for a theory of consciousness-raising in the 90s during a psychology theory class, part of the social work program at Springfield College. This text forged a path of hope not only for my career as an effective clinician, but also as a creator of a psychological theory. It articulates what my own life's path had already taught me, and proves beyond doubt that human beings are capable of change, and that the most profound vehicle for change is consciousness-raising.

I, along with many others in the field of evolutionary thinking, regard Evolutionary and Futurist Barbara Marx Hubbard as a leader in the field of evolution and a key center of influence for the vision of a positive future. Her devotion to the work of assisting the evolutionary process is evident with her writings, teachings, and most recently her promotion of the *Birth of the New Humanity (December 2012).* Thank you, Barbara, for making my heart sing, influencing my work, and creating an atmosphere that is ripe for this new theory of psychology.

Special thanks to Dr. Thomas Moore for all his work, for the wonderful week-long summer workshop on the Cape that really inspired me to get writing. I found renewed inspiration in his recent article in *Spirituality & Health* when he proclaimed that study and scholarly pursuits are spiritual activities! Hurray! Hours of reading, writing, researching, and learning while sitting up straight, maintaining focus, assimilating concepts, and preparing *the message* can certainly be considered no less than personal and collective consciousness-raising activities.

Special thanks to all my teachers along the way. Patrick DeChello, Ph.D., founder of D&S Associates, LLC was my advisor, intern supervisor *and* favorite professor at Springfield College. Today he continues to not only be a mentor, but also produced and promoted my first workshop for professionals, *Spirituality and Psychology: Are They Really Separate?* His friendship and faith in my work continue to inspire me. Website: dandsaccociates.net

There can be no substitute for the *Work* we do on ourselves, in person, with a spiritual teacher. I am most grateful to Gene Ang, Ph.D, a Yale trained neurobiologist who has devoted his life to the exploration, facilitation, and tutoring of Energy Medicine and the Human Energy System. Dr. Ang has a healing practice in Westlake Village, California. He facilitates an ever-expanding array of healing techniques, hosts workshops throughout the United States, and leads Sacred Travel groups to healing centers worldwide. I have attended numerous workshops including two in Sedona, AZ. I am eternally grateful that he introduced me to The Reconnection®, DNA activation exercises, and all the latest state-of-the-art and divinely inspired energy-healing modalities. Website: geneang.com

My immediate gratitude goes to my newest angel, editor Linda Moore, of Cambridge Project Resources in Cambridge, NY. She was divinely inspired to answer my Connecticut-based Craigslist ad in the nick of time, just as I was giving up on finding help. (Being from rural upstate NY, she recalls not understanding why she was

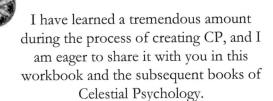

I have learned a tremendous amount during the process of creating CP, and I am eager to share it with you in this workbook and the subsequent books of Celestial Psychology.

even bothering to check CT!) Her support and encouragement to prepare "a manuscript we can both be proud of" is beyond measure—it's priceless. Website: cambridgeprojectresources.com

By choosing to read this book, whether you actually do the exercises or not, I know your journey into consciousness-raising has already begun. Whether you are a novice to all this or an experienced practitioner or facilitator of any of the healing arts, I am confident your journey into consciousness-raising will be enhanced by what you learn in the pages ahead, much like mine was during the course of learning and discovery while writing them.

I thank you in advance for reading these pages. I am honored to share a part your journey, and I honor you for doing the *Holy Work* of consciousness-raising with *Celestial Psychology*®.

Smiles and Blessings,

Celeste Emelia Mattingly, LCSW
celestialpsychology.com

Invitation

In Chapter One, you will see that I refer to this workbook as a journey, an adventure, a path, and a historical excursion. It is an exciting journey into uncharted territories. Seminal ideas and never-before presented exercises for consciousness-raising have been designed to improve QOL, enhance luminosity, and ignite an evolutionary flame. The path is meticulously laid out to provide a crescendo of increased knowledge, mastery over self, and an undeniable connection- elevating mind and body to spirit.

I invite you to follow the recommendations below to the best of your ability and join me on this journey using this workbook as your guide.

Suggestions and Recommendations

In order to get the most out of your journey through this workbook, I recommend the following:

First, (as odd as it may seem), I recommend starting at the back of the book and familiarizing yourself with the glossary of terms. The terms have been compiled by consulting different sources, synthesizing the information, and presenting them according to *Celestial Psychology*®. Many of the terms are more like footnotes, and are designed to enhance your experience, and better prepare you for the crescendo of awakening that may occur with completion of the final chapters.

Next, in order to further your journey, I recommend taking a quick read through the chapters, and then spending approximately one week focused on each chapter in the order they are presented. Read each chapter daily and follow the instructions for the exercises to the best of your ability. If at any time you suspect that you are getting too high, please stop for a day or two and ground yourself with some gardening, exercise, or TV, and eat some root vegetables or red meat. Once you have completed the weekly routine, incorporate your favorite aspects and exercises from each chapter for quick daily review.

> Working on the chakras in combination with their parallel psychological concepts provides a more expedient and efficacious potential to become self-actualized.

If possible, record your voice repeating the affirmations, as this is a powerful way to reach the subconscious mind and access the astral manifestation plane. Limit your daily journaling. Fifteen minutes per day will keep the work fresh and spontaneous. Whenever possible, work with a mentor, therapist, or a friend.

I have included numerous references and resources within each chapter, and I encourage you to learn more about these authors by reading their books, visiting their websites, signing up for their newsletters, and attending their workshops.

Practicing the techniques in this workbook is an ascendance through the chakra system. Throughout, I have combined the concepts of one or two corresponding psychological theories with exercises designed to awaken each related chakra. This combination of insightful concepts and powerful exercises will help you create profound and lasting change—a shift in consciousness. As you experience this shift, you may awaken to the realization that you are also assisting the species as a whole to shift to higher consciousness, thus assisting evolution itself.

Working on the chakras in combination with their parallel psychological concepts provides a more expedient and efficacious potential to become self-actualized. You will have the tools to become a master and to understand the infinite power of thought, a co-creator not only of your own life, but of the universe itself.

To spark your evolutionary flame, each chapter features an evolutionary affirmation with an image of a fish.

By doing the Holy Work of consciousness-raising, we are collectively being propelled toward a bright and glorious future, thereby ensuring we will develop our ethereal lungs and wings in order to survive.

Fish were the first species to develop backbone, and there is a growing consensus they were the precursors of birds. Scientists are discovering definitive links between fish scales and feathers. The image of a fish flopping about in a muddy pool of drying primordial soup, developing its gills into lungs and its scales into feathers, is becoming an evolutionary archetype for our species at this time of the Shift. We are those fish, and as we realize this, our enthusiasm for this work accelerates.

While doing the exercises in each chapter, be mindful that you are contributing to the evolution of our species! By doing the Holy Work of consciousness-raising, we are collectively being propelled toward a bright and glorious future, thereby ensuring we will develop our ethereal lungs and wings in order to survive.

I selected yoga poses for each chapter based on my research of websites too numerous to mention. Many yoga sites provide instructions if you are not familiar with the poses or need a refresher. I urge you to study with a certified yoga teacher to ensure the best experience.

I teach various exercises in my Spiritual Empowerment classes. One of these is the basic T'ai Chi Stance, known as the water position, and it is great to use whenever possible. For example, I recommend dropping into the stance while waiting in line, washing dishes, walking, or doing other exercises such as the energy work warm-up below.

Basic T'ai Chi Stance—Water Position

Place feet shoulder width apart, toes pointing forward, knees slightly bent, shoulders relaxed, tummy tight, buttocks tucked in, elbows tucked at side, and spine stretched up. Hold a T'ai chi ball at chi center.

Visualize a beach ball in your hands. Experience the magnetism in your palms. Practice feeling the energy in your hands by cupping them and keeping your fingers stiff. Practice the slinky, the silly-putty and the taffy-pull techniques for activating healing energy recommended by Dr. Eric Pearl in *The Reconnection*.

Prior to each class, we warm up with a series of exercises as taught by Dr. Gene Ang. These exercises are designed to stimulate the energetic body, and I recommend practicing this warm-up before each chapter's exercises, or any form of therapeutic energy work or meditation. A recommendation is to do a set of 12 of each exercise, incorporating the water position (basic T'ai Chi stance) as much as possible.

Energy Work Warm-up

1. **Eye roll.** Stand in the water position. Start with your eyes wide open. Imagine a clock in front of you at eye level. Begin by focusing on the 12. Keep your eyes wide open, your head stationery, and your chin level with the floor as you complete 12 clockwise and then 12 counterclockwise circles. Complete each circle within 3 to 5 seconds.

2. **Neck twist.** Keep your chin level with the floor as you slowly turn your head toward your left shoulder. Look over your left shoulder, twisting back as far as possible. Slowly turn your head back to center, and then to the right to look over your right shoulder, twisting back as far as possible. Slowly turn your head back to center. This is one set. Complete 12 sets.

3. **Waist stretch.** Raise your left arm over your head and gently bend at the waist to the right. Feel the stretch along your left side. Count to 7 as you continue the stretch and loosely shake

your dangling right arm to release tension. Then reverse and raise your right arm over your head, gently stretching at the waist to the left. Feel the stretch along your right side. Count to 7 while stretching and loosely shaking your dangling left arm to release tension. This is one set. Complete 12 sets.

4. **Hip rotation**. Place your hands on your hips and rotate your hips with a hula-hoop motion. Complete 12 circles to the left, and then 12 circles to the right.

5. **Bouncing or stepping in place**. Jump up 50 times, lifting off the ground about three inches if you are in good shape. Otherwise, take 100 steps, lifting your feet an exaggerated six inches without strain.

6. **Shoulder rotation**. With arms relaxed at your sides, lift your shoulders in a circular motion. Start by creating 12 circles backward, and then complete 12 circles forward.

7. **Elbow extension**. Begin with arms slightly raised forward and curled at the elbows. Gently snap your arms out with your palms up. Then curl them back up. Complete 12 times.

8. **Wrist roll**. With arms slightly extended forward roll your wrists in a circular motion. First complete 12 circles in an outward direction, and then 12 circles in an inward direction.

9. **Hand shake**. With arms slightly raised forward and curled at the elbows, gently snap them forward with palms down and fingers snapping out (as if shaking off water). Then curl them back up. Complete the motion 12 times.

10. **Leg kicks**. Stand on your right foot and gently kick your left foot forward from the knee. Complete 12 kicks with the left foot, and then reverse for 12 kicks with the right foot.*

11. **Ankle twist**. Stand on your right foot. Raise your left foot about six inches and rotate at the ankle in an outward circle 12 times. Switch. Stand on your left foot, rotate your right foot at the ankle in an outward circle 12 times. Switch feet again and rotate in an inward motion 12 times each foot.*

12. **Foot flex**. Stand on your right foot. Raise your left up and down at the ankle 12 times. Switch feet and repeat 12 times.*

*If necessary, hold on to something to maintain your balance, and keep your eyes looking to the horizon. In time, you will be able to balance yourself naturally, especially as you develop your energetic body.

> For many of us, despite our hard work, it seems like nothing is happening. Please don't get discouraged, because something is always happening beyond what we can see, feel or believe. This *Work always* produces results beyond the veil of our human perception. It is a lifelong process—we are all works in progress. So, relax; do what moves you to the best of your ability; and trust. It's all in divine order.

As you read and practice, please keep in mind that the goal of any good path for awakening is to incorporate the teachings and make them our own. Some of the exercises may not be to your liking, so take what you need and leave the rest. The truth is that miracles, awakenings, and shifts in consciousness can happen in the blink of an eye by mere acknowledgment. For many of us, despite our hard work, it seems like nothing is happening. Please don't get discouraged, because something is always happening beyond what we can see, feel or believe. This *Work always* produces results beyond the veil of our human perception. It is a lifelong process—we are all works in progress. So, relax, do what moves you to the best of your ability, and trust—-it's all in divine order.

If you are a teacher or practitioner of any healing arts, I hope you will incorporate this workbook into your practices.

It is my fondest hope that I will hear from you. I welcome your feedback, as research is paramount to launching any new theory. My websites are listed in the front pages of the book. Remember to practice smiling, and knowing that the *Force is always with you* on your journey. ✸

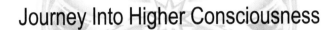

CHAPTER 1

Journey Into Higher Consciousness

This workbook is an exciting experiential adventure into consciousness-raising to improve quality of life (QOL). It is a journey into uncharted territory, and its main path is forged with a strikingly parallel and unprecedented analysis of the human chakra system and the historical development of psychological theories. It begins with a look at how Freudian psychoanalysis, considered the first wave of psychology, provides the roots of all consciousness-raising, just as chakra one provides the roots for the whole chakra system. Traveling upward through each chakra and chronologically through the historical development of psychological theory provides new and insightful awareness. Arriving at chakra seven, we see the stunning parallel to Celestial Psychology® and are introduced to the epoch-making introduction of a fifth wave of psychology—Conscious Evolutionary Psychology.

The exercises, visualizations, meditations, affirmations, and forward-thinking concepts presented in this workbook guide you on a step-by-step ascent into higher consciousness. It is here that we discover that psychology has paved the way for Oneness in the West, and how science is validating the reality of spirituality as well. With the

On this journey, I will introduce you to five amazing postulates, each of which has the power to elevate your thinking. When combined, they have been described as "mind-blowing."

exercises and concepts, we experience how inextricably woven psychology and spirituality have always been, thereby proving as we study one, we are actually studying the other; when combined into experiential exercises, the results are astounding.

The journey through this workbook will enhance your ability to improve yourself, and provide impetus to easily and joyously say, "Yes!" to your own spiritual empowerment and to our collective responsibility to contribute to the evolution of the species.

On this journey, I will introduce you to five amazing postulates, each of which has the power to elevate your thinking. When combined, they have been described as "mind-blowing."

1. Western acceptance of the chakra system has been paved inadvertently by psychological theory as it has matured to the present day.
2. Starting with Freudian psychology and ending with present-day psychology, psychological theory has evolved with a startlingly parallel correspondence to the human chakra system.
3. The individual's work of raising consciousness corresponds with the collective, and therefore the evolution of the species.
4. Psychological theory has functioned as a spiral of compounding knowledge to raise the collective unconscious in a way that excitingly brings humanity to its crown chakra, the noosphere.
5. Psychology itself is evolving (pun intended) into its fifth and possibly last wave of psychological theory. I am naming this fifth wave "Conscious Evolutionary Psychology," with Celestial Psychology as its primary defining theoretical framework.

We will explore and experience the fascinating correlation between the colorful, spinning, healing vortices of the chakra system and the increasing healing capabilities of psychology and psychological theories over the past 100 years. The following diagram outlines this correlation.

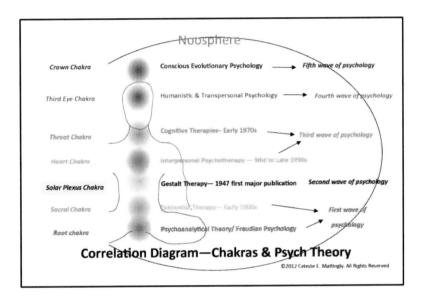

Correlation Diagram—Chakras & Psych Theory

©2012 Celeste E. Mattingly. All Rights Reserved

It is impossible to take this journey, this examination of the historical development of psychology, without an evolutionary perspective, also known as evolutionary eyes. Viewing the historical development of psychology through evolutionary eyes shows us that because psychology has always been about raising consciousness, it is inevitable that as psychological theory developed the consciousness of psychology itself would have to raise. Even more stunning is the discovery that higher consciousness is revealing *itself* through the gradual awakening of our collective minds.

The journey in this workbook proves that psychological theory has prepared us as individuals for Oneness. The literal meaning of the word psychology is *study of the soul,* and since its inception, the meaning of psyche has been limited (or some would say inhibited) to the mind. Now as we collectively awaken and eclectically merge all the knowledge our minds have ever gathered about the mind, science, spirituality, consciousness, and psychology, we discover that in so doing, we have been learning about Soul. We can call it whatever we want—energy, God, the Creator, the Source, the One, or the Force as it was called in the famous movie Star Wars—it is all the same.

This brings us to another realization: because we are studying Creation or Soul when we study psychology and consciousness, we are also studying evolution! Carter Phipps, in his 2012 exciting new release, *Evolutionaries: Unlocking the Spiritual and Cultural Potential of Science's Greatest Idea,* points out, "interpretation of evolutionary science is evolving in ways that will have a significant effect on how we make meaning in the coming decades and centuries."[1] We will see on our journey that "how we make meaning" is a theme that runs through all psychological theoretical approaches.

"It is almost as if a new form of spiritual intuition is dawning upon those with the inner eyesight to perceive it. Evolutionaries often report that this internal evolutionary timescape…can also arise suddenly in consciousness, analogous to the flash of insight characteristic of a spiritual awakening…. Awakening to a felt sense of the past and the future as much vaster than ever considered before, the individual nature of his or her, own consciousness, of culture, of life, and even of the cosmos itself.
The spell of solidity is broken deep in the recesses of the psyche and a new vision of an evolving world pours forth, an epiphany not just of unity and oneness but of movement and temporality."
—**Carter Phipps**

At the conclusion of our journey through this workbook, you will have the means to improve your QOL beyond your wildest dreams. The exercises have the potential to prepare your body, mind, and spirit to hold new energetic frequencies and to experience heightened states of awareness, spiritual awakenings, and perhaps enlightenment. The exciting original ideas can provide you with a new kind of spirituality where you may come to know your divinity through your personal consciousness-raising, rather than externally-driven authoritative dogma.

You will have the means to be forever changed. And the opportunity to remain forever changing.

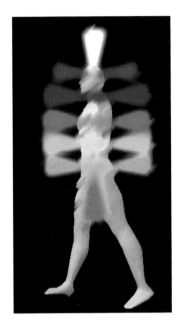

CHAPTER 2

What is the Human Chakra System?

Chakras are transformation stations! They are energetic force fields in which consciousness, consisting of spiritual, psychological, and physical qualities, merge, blend, and transform into utilizable energy. Chakras are included within the broader Human Energy System (HES), whose elements such as layers, meridians, cords, and cord bundles.

Chakra in Sanskrit means *wheel* or *disk*. These disks or wheels gather and absorb or dispel and disseminate, thereby managing energetic information by spinning in vortex formations. It is generally taught that a clockwise (the clock being positioned on the front of the body) spin is gathering and a counterclockwise spin is disseminating or clearing; and that the faster the spin, the healthier the individual. Chakras are the spinning vortices of prana or life energy that cannot been seen by most people, or found in autopsies, however, they have been measured with electromyography (electrical testing of the body) and documented with Kirlian photography, which captures energetic/electrical emissions or aura of a person or object.

There are numerous depictions of the chakras, but most artists concur a lotus with petals acting as the spokes of the wheel is the best representation. For example, the first chakra is a four-petal lotus and the fifth chakra is a sixteen-petal lotus. The petals contribute to the varying intensity and direction each chakra spins. The direction of the spin and its intensity can be activated by focusing one's attention and intent on them, especially with a combination of exercises, such as repeating affirmations or utilizing visualization, while meditating, practicing yoga or the martial arts t'ai chi or qigong. With the help of its petals, each chakra collects and emits energy in the form of light (especially sunlight) color vibrations: electromagnetic, cosmic, gamma, infrared, micro, and long and short radio waves.

> The first chakra is a four-petal lotus and the fifth chakra is a sixteen-petal lotus. The petals contribute to the varying intensity and direction each chakra spins. The direction of the spin and its intensity can be activated by focusing one's attention and intent on them.

The chakras are connected energetically to the nerve ganglia of the spinal cord. These vortices of moving energies stimulate the endocrine glands to secrete hormones into the blood stream.

Together with the subtle body and its layers of consciousness, the chakras are associated with the metaphysical, the psyche, or consciousness. Each chakra has a specific connection to our mental, emotional, spiritual, and physical beings. As we go through this workbook, we will see the direct impact the chakras have, learn how they can improve our quality of life (QOL) and experience them as transformation stations.

Chakras govern areas of human endeavor as well as qualities of the human psyche. For instance, each chakra is thought to govern every individual's rights *to have, to feel, to know*, etc. And each chakra has associated positive and negative characteristics that govern the individual's personality or psyche. There is a striking commonality among the different systems that have developed over time immemorial that can only lead one to marvel over the validity of these interpretations. During our journey, we will take an in-depth look at the positive and negative archetypes, beautifully articulated by Ambika Wauters in her book, *The Book of Chakras: Discover the Hidden Forces Within You*. Each workbook chapter devoted to the chakras includes her comprehensive and thought-provoking list of qualities and attributes. I highly recommend adding this exquisite, illustrated book to your library.

Each chakra has an associated seed sound, a sound vibration corresponding to its particular area of the body. Chanting the seed sound while holding the mudra, or posture, associated with each chakra is an effective way to experience the activity or vibration of each. During my classes, we inhale deeply to chant the sound three times for seven to ten breaths. Then, using the room's sound system, I play chakra music from Baird Hersey's fantastic mind-expanding album, *Waking the Cobra*. At times, while free-form chanting the seed sound, some participants have near out-of-body experiences!

Each chakra has a corresponding musical note, different from the seed sound. Spiritual teachers and mystics have long held that the psychic spine of the chakra system can be played as a flute-like or reed instrument by the *winds* of spirit blowing through them.

Each chakra has a corresponding musical note, different from the seed sound. Spiritual teachers and mystics have long held that the psychic spine of the chakra system can be played as a flute-like or reed instrument by the *winds* of spirit blowing through them.

This workbook's front cover and diagrams illustrate each chakra's corresponding color. These colors are the primary colors of the rainbow. Most literature supports the rainbow as the bridge between the material and spiritual, or as we shall see later, the bridge into the noosphere from the biosphere, or more simply, a rainbow-bridge into higher consciousness.

It is not known exactly when or how the chakra system came to be known. References are found as far back as the ancient Vedic records, the oldest scriptures of Hinduism, and, according to historians, perhaps as early as 4500 BC. The chakra system is generally attributed to Hindu traditions, although Buddhism has carried it to modernity as well. There are also references to chakra systems in Chinese, Jewish

"The word chakra literally means 'disk.' How fitting that in modern times, disks are the common storage unit of programmed information. We can use this analogy and think of chakras as floppy disks that contain vital programs."
—Anodea Judith

Kabbalah (Ten Sefirot Emanations), and Islamic (thirteen-chakra system) mysticism. Ancient Native American and indigenous peoples worldwide knew them as circles of light. Egyptian healing arts included activating a thirteen-chakra system, with which practitioners perfected aromatherapy and color therapy. Both therapies are gaining popularity today. Although there are many differing systems and models for the chakras themselves, there are characteristics common to all ancient and contemporary systems, as described by Anodea Judith[2], Ambika Wauters, Caroline Myss, Zachary Selig and others.

Currently, there is no universal standard or model of the chakra system. As we have seen, some systems claim as many as thirteen major and hundreds of smaller chakras, the smaller ones corresponding to joints and acupuncture points of the body. Yet, most systems, especially in the Western world, agree there are seven major or primary chakras. We will consider these seven chakras throughout this workbook.

We will review each chakra's parallel correspondence to its psychological theoretical counterpart, and also get to know each chakra's associated color, sound, element, and other provocative qualities. We will get to know the physical, mental, emotional, and spiritual connections that are capable of transforming us and improving our quality of life, our QOL.

Learning to acknowledge,

The chakra system of the human subtle body has gradually gained mainstream acceptance over the last century. It is becoming known as integral to the health and well-being of all individuals, society, and the species as a whole.

clear, balance, and utilize these frequencies or energies to heal ourselves, each other, and the planet is paramount in these critical times. Activating or awakening our light bodies by way of our chakras increases energy level, improves QOL, prepares the ethereal or celestial body for life after death and, possibly, for the next incarnation or for inter-dimensional universal existence. As we shift into the new dawn of awareness and the noosphere opens up, maintaining optimal chakra health will become second nature to us.

The Introduction of Chakras Into Psychology

The chakra system of the human subtle body has gradually gained mainstream acceptance over the last century. It is becoming known as integral to the health and well-being of all individuals, society, and the species as a whole. The idea of energy as a system in the body, like a skeletal or nervous system, was first recognized by psychiatry in the mid-1930s.

Wilhelm Reich, M.D. (March 24, 1897–November 3, 1957) is credited with first introducing the idea of *energy* circulating through the body, although it was not identified as the chakra system. Reich was born and raised in Austria, and after graduating from the University of Vienna in 1922, he became a director in Sigmund Freud's

Psychoanalytic Polyclinic. His early work as a psychoanalyst was well received, and today there are schools of Reichian therapy, a number of research laboratories, and an American College of Orgonomy (ACO).

It was, however, Reich's contentious discovery of orgone (energy absorbed by organic matter) and his invention of the orgone energy accumulator in the late 1930s that threatened his credibility so much that his mental health suffered. He became paranoid and could not defend his discoveries to the medical community. The orgone accumulators were phone booth-shaped boxes made mostly of wood and various metals. Purportedly, the boxes generated healing and cured disease by gathering and accumulating orgone as patients sat inside them. The concept gained popularity, and the boxes were sold and rented for huge costs. In 1954, the FDA sued Reich for false claims. He continued to promote his orgone accumulators, and was subsequently imprisoned by the US government, which reportedly seized and burned many of his books. He died in prison in 1957. Dubbed the most controversial figure in psychiatry, Reich is considered a martyr and hero by many of his followers.

In one of his most revolutionary publications, *The Bion Experiments on the Origin of Life*, Reich documented his ability to produce a visible blue-gray shimmering luminous vapor that would permeate a room and promote healing.

Reich's studies, discoveries, and life's work may prove to be the first, although elementary, scientific proof that the vital life force—t'ai chi, prana, ether, or Kundalini is real. There is no doubt, however, that he was the first Western physician to correlate this knowledge to the mental, emotional, and physical states of man. He developed specific techniques for uncovering unconscious blockages to move the energy around and release disease-causing negative and stuck states. His profound understanding of human nature acquired as a student of Freud, combined with his genius (or madness?) made his work very effective. He used physical exercises resembling yoga and vocal exercises that resemble today's sound healing techniques.

In one of his most revolutionary publications, *The Bion Experiments on the Origin of Life*, Reich documented his ability to produce a visible blue-gray shimmering luminous vapor that would permeate a room and promote healing. His work is considered by many to be truly visionary. Today, orgonomy is considered a science by The American College of Orgonomy, which was founded in 1968, at Reich's request, by Dr. Elsworth F. Baker, MD. Reich hoped his work would be carried on. Surely, ACO's continued success and biopsychiatric treatment established as a viable modality would have exceeded his hopes. Orgonomy is considered a natural approach with applications not only to psychiatry and biology but also to general medical practices and sociology.

The most renowned student and colleague of Reich is John Pierrakos, MD, PhD (1921–). He worked closely with Reich, first as a patient, then as a student, and then later as a colleague for many years. He believes in the essence of Reich's work, yet Pierrakos admits he never

> Lowen and Pierrakos developed bioenergetics—a system for working with the human energy flow, based on what they had learned about energy and character defenses while working with Reich.

saw the shimmering luminous vapors of orgone the way Reich did. In a short online autobiography[3] he writes, "When I told him I wanted to see orgone energy, he took me down to his basement laboratory and put me in the orgone accumulator. I saw strange things—spiral movements, rays and foglike masses—I thought something was wrong with my eyes; I was disappointed. My scientific training in medical school hadn't prepared me for an experience like that!"

Pierrakos began a private practice with a fellow Reichian, Alexander Lowen, around the time Reich began having difficulties with the law and the FDA. Together, Lowen and Pierrakos developed bioenergetics—a system for working with the human energy flow, based on what they had learned about energy and character defenses while working with Reich. "It was very exciting to experiment with new techniques and concepts. We worked from the feet up and the head down, grounding the personality both energetically and mentally."[4]

Bioenergetics is most commonly understood to be the biochemical study of the cellular process, and it is a field of biochemistry. However, to distinguish it as a psychotherapeutic process, some practitioners and schools refer to it as bioenergetic analysis. The basic premise is that body and mind are not separate and they need to be understood as integral to their respective functions. Breathing techniques, such as staccato breathing, and grounding through the feet and legs distinguish it from the earlier schools of Reichian therapy.

Pierrakos grew unhappy with the work of bioenergetics, believing that it was missing something. When he met Eva Broch (1915–1979), a Vienna-born medium and spiritual guide, he immediately understood

"I yearn to see Core Energetics blossom in many more ways in order to help unify the split between psychology, religion, science, and personal life. My work is to reach the depth of a person's entirety. To help that person open up, transform–**move**!"[5]

—**John Pierrakos**

the missing something was spirituality. Eva was beautiful, vibrantly alive, and intent on helping people improve their lives. Pierrakos began taking creative, integrative, and spiritual counseling from Eva's guide, named *The Guide*. Eva and John quickly realized how truly parallel their work was, and they fell in love and married in 1971. He helped her develop *The Pathwork for Self-Transformation*, by incorporating psychological aspects into her spiritual work, and she helped him incorporate spirituality into his practice. She died of cancer in 1979, just as they were founding the Institute of Core Energetics, an organization dedicated to inspiring people to transform themselves— to open up and circulate their energy and improve their physical and mental health by *moving*.

Currently called The Institute of Core Energetics International, it is located in New York City and offers a full curriculum as well as a number of professional workshops focused on the combination of psychoanalysis, bioenergetics, and *The Pathwork*. Pierrakos is also the author of *Core Energetics: Developing the Capacity to Love and Heal* and *Eros, Love, and Sexuality: The Forces that Unify Men and Women.*

Barbara Brennan, PhD, a former NASA physicist, is another major contributor to bringing the idea of a circulating HES into mainstream medicine and alternative healing. For the last thirty years, Dr. Brennan, has dedicated her life to the human energy field. Her best-selling books, *Hands of Light, Light Emerging,* and the *Seeds of the Spirit* book series, have furthered worldwide acceptance that energy, commonly called the aura or auric field, can be seen and manipulated—that the orgone of Wilhelm Reich's world is, in fact, quite real.

> Brennan's system, based on "the living dynamics of our Human Energy-Consciousness System," and combining "hands-on healing techniques with spiritual and psychological processes," transforms and brings into balance all aspects of one's life.

She founded the Barbara Brennan School of Healing in 1982, which offers baccalaureate degrees and certification programs in Brennan Healing Science. Brennan's system, based on "the living dynamics of our Human Energy-Consciousness System," combines "hands-on healing techniques with spiritual and psychological processes,"[6] transforms and brings into balance all aspects of one's life. Her work with the human energy field is used as the standard of healing with energy and the chakras.

> All over the modern world, human beings are waking up to *energy* and higher consciousness, and they are clearing and balancing their chakras in record numbers.

Today's leading authority on chakras and their psychological connection is, undoubtedly, Anodea Judith, Ph.D. Her best-selling (over 200,000 copies sold) book, *Wheels of Life: A User's Guide to the Chakra System* has been translated into fifteen languages, and is considered the standard for chakra knowledge. In 1997, after three decades of teaching a popular workshop, "Psychology and the Chakra System as a Path to the Self," she published *Eastern Body, Western Mind: Psychology and the Chakra System as a Path to the Self.* This comprehensive 488-page book is used as a text in many healing schools and a number of universities. Judith has brilliantly organized this material in a way that fosters deep learning and transformation. She merged her interpretations of the chakras with Western psychology, covering everything from trauma and abuse to Jung's transcendent function. In 1999, she founded, and continues to direct, *Sacred Centers* to promote her teachings. Judith's center offers certification programs for healing practices as well as community events focused on the individual and society's push toward transformation and, ultimately, evolution.

All over the modern world, human beings are waking up to *energy* and higher consciousness, and they are clearing and balancing their chakras in record numbers. There are many different methods to activate the transforming capabilities of the chakras. Yoga (meaning to literally *yoke* energy to the divine), t'ai chi, qigong, martial arts, and a myriad of breathing and meditation techniques are gaining popularity exponentially. Classes and workshops are offered in many mainstream hospitals and alcohol and drug treatment centers. Access to transformative teachings is paramount and timely as our health and the health of the planet are drastically compromised by toxic chemicals, impurities, pollutants, and especially our own negative thinking.

Scientists and allopathic medicine practitioners are often at a loss as solar flares and genetically modified foods disfigure our environment and attack our bodies. Thankfully, alternative medical approaches are on the rise to combat this growing crisis. Gaining awareness and understanding of the chakra system, our vital energy source, is becoming mainstream and therapeutic techniques are more widely available to assist individuals and practitioners from all disciplines to wake up to higher consciousness—to better mental, physical, mental, and emotional health.

"The chakra system describes the energetic structure through which we organize our life force. By understanding this internal arrangement, we can understand our defenses and needs, and learn how to restore balance. The chakra system is every bit as valid as any psychological theory, and I feel, far more versatile—one that is capable of spanning mind, body, and spirit. I invite you to explore it with me and thereby deepen your own healing process."[7]

—Anodea Judith

I, too, invite you to explore, practice, and incorporate the wisdom presented in this workbook. In the quote above, Judith declares psychological theory a valid system, perhaps not as valid or versatile as the chakra system. However, the discovery of the correlation between the historical development of psychological theory and the chakras supports the validity and versatility of the work in this workbook.

CHAPTER 3

Chakras – Energy System
Transformation Stations

Chakra One

Muladhara
Root Support

Psychoanalytical Theory and Chakra One

The first chakra is named Muladhara. *Mula* in Sanskrit means "foundation" and *adhara* means "support." Located at the base of the spine or perineum, it connects to the nervous system at the coccygeal plexus, which includes sacral and pelvic nerves. Muladhara extends downward from the spine into the ground, deep into the earth, and it is our root chakra. Muladhara forms the foundation for the entire human chakra system. It represents our relationship with our physical bodies and the material world, and it is related to the element earth. The root chakra influences our careers and finances, and grounds us in physical existence. When balanced, its energy helps us to blend the physical and spiritual. Muladhara aids our ability to make money, find security, and eliminate what is no longer needed for growth. Because Muladhara governs the right *to have* and the right *to be here*, we enjoy physical existence when it is balanced. We unequivocally know that we belong, we are safe, and, as in Maslow's hierarchy, our basic needs are being met.

Sigmund Freud (1856–1939) is widely accepted as the father of Western psychology, and psychoanalytic and psychodynamic theories are regarded as the first wave of psychological theories. The fundamental technique of Freud's psychoanalytic therapy is the practice of free association, which he made popular in the late 1800s. Free association was psychology's first consciousness-raising technique, and it remains the basis of all healing and conscious endeavors to improve ourselves. Free association is the process in which a patient is encouraged to verbalize whatever is on his or her mind—honestly, freely, and without censure. In order to find relief from symptoms, especially generalized anxiety and what Freud considered pregenital fixations, patients were encouraged to ramble, ignoring content concerns, sharing secrets, childhood memories and dreams, while the analyst takes notes.

Chakra one balancing and psychoanalysis teaches us that once we have our roots firmly planted and we are grounded, we will have health, vitality, stability, prosperity, and good quality of life.

Victorians of that prim and proper era were particularly reluctant to share their thoughts, darkest fantasies, and, painful memories. However, Freud's techniques allowed the patient to trust him and to learn to feel safe. Patients were required to lie on a couch for comfort and deep relaxation. They did not face the psychoanalyst in order to avoid any interference in the process. If the patient experienced resistance, the trained psychoanalyst would make suggestions that may or may not resonate with the patient, thereby freeing his or her subconscious.

Free association may sound simple, but it can be especially daunting for individuals with repressed memories resulting from a trauma of any sort. Telling a therapist everything that comes to mind, whether from one's waking life, or from one's dream life, remains as much a challenge, in today's world as it was for the Victorians. Today, most therapists favor comfortable seating for their clients. However, like Freud, most contemporary psychoanalysts find it important not to face a client[8] directly, hopefully making it easier for the client to share his or her thoughts without censoring them first.

Letting go of pre-conceived notions of self and sharing innermost thoughts demand that a client set aside fears of vulnerability and emotional discomfort and muster considerable amounts of trust, courage, and defenselessness. It takes the skill of a trained psychoanalyst to facilitate this process with assurances of no reprisal, judgment, or repercussion. Especially when treating clients with histories of trauma it is imperative to provide an atmosphere of safety. This process marks the beginning of a patient's ability to deliberately and consciously examine his or her own mind for the purpose of reducing neurosis, or in contemporary terms, to improve his or her QOL. Simply, we can't pursue happiness if we do not know what is making us unhappy.

> The conscious mind may be compared to a fountain playing in the sun and falling back into the great subterranean pool of subconscious from which it rises.
> **–Sigmund Freud**

Free association is an act of consciousness-raising—making conscious what is unconscious. Prochaska and Norcross state, "Freud, the intra-psychic master…decided that the desirable content of psychoanalysis—the therapeutic goal—was to make the unconscious conscious."[9] Making conscious what is unconscious is still considered the most desirable outcome of psychoanalysis. It is the logical basis for consciousness-raising, and it corresponds with the first chakra because it is truly the root of analysis. Classical psychoanalytical therapy is the foundation of psychology that has developed over the past one hundred years, just as the first chakra, Muladhara, is the root of the body's chakra system.

With psychoanalytical therapy, we have a means to make changes and better our lives through awakenings, insight, and interpretation.

Chakra one analysis and balancing work teaches us that once we have our roots firmly planted and we are grounded, we will have health, vitality, stability, prosperity, and good quality of life; our QOL will be solid, we will fully comprehend our rights to be here and to have safety, security, self-grounding, and connectedness.

The first chakra focuses on the material world and encourages trust, just as the process of free association promotes trusting. Survival is the primary theme of the first chakra and a fundamental of the psychoanalytical process. Survival is the ability and willingness to keep oneself alive and well. Feeling safe and secure in one's life, is the automatic secondary theme which derives from being successful at survival. Patients learn to recognize that support is available when the therapist maintains unconditional positive regard for them and is able to stay present and empathetic through the dredging of the patient's subconscious.

Muladhara generates support through relationships, and finances. Working through fight or flight toward balanced responses to trauma is a building block of both psychotherapy and chakra balancing. Knowing we are strongly connected to the earth and our tribes (our affiliation groups—biological family, co-workers, peers, friends, etc.), and trusting all will be well are outcomes of both processes. When we must face the inevitability of life's chaos, psychotherapy and chakra balancing educate us as to how to live with change. A positive worldview, a belief in the goodness of life, and the ability to free-associate what is unconscious are by-products of a solid first chakra and good mental health. A sincere commitment to make conscious what is unconscious and a strong first chakra help us live as the wheat—bending and swaying through life's challenges, but standing straight and strong when the storm has passed. ✸

Classical psychoanalytical therapy is the foundation of psychology that has developed over the past one hundred years, just as the first chakra, Muladhara, is the root of the body's chakra system.

Physiological Signs of Chakra One Imbalance

The physical areas of the body governed by the first chakra are the solid parts of the body such as skeletal system (bones) and teeth and lower body (feet, ankles, knees, legs, back and especially sciatic area). Problems associated with these physical areas are regarded as first chakra blockage. Digestive system problems, especially with the bowel, colon, and rectum, such as, chronic diarrhea, constipation, and irritable bowel syndrome and problems with blood (high blood pressure) and immune systems (frequent illness) are other common physiological presentations. Problems with the nervous system, adrenals (fatigue), muscles, and skin can often be corrected with first chakra balancing and/or clearing.

Psychological Signs of Chakra One Imbalance

Ineffectiveness at meeting basic human needs, eating disorders, dissociative disorders, OCD, depression, addictions, and hoarding may reflect chakra one imbalance. Symptoms include being uncomfortable in one's own skin and lacking a sense of belonging or fitting in. Fears such as fear of abandonment, or fear that the child personality will override the adult may develop. Problems with unfinished family business, "tribes," (beliefs or connections), or poor finances may present themselves.

Therapeutic Focus

Combine chakra-balancing exercises with a developing trust in the clinician's positive regard (and the goodwill of others in our lives) and the therapeutic process itself. Utilize free association and speaking one's mind to access the subconscious and do so without fear. Encourage reconnection with the body through physical activity, especially the chakra exercises presented here. Exploration of earliest childhood memories, especially, with mother, is encouraged in psychoanalytical therapy and first chakra work.

Notes

_____

_____

_____

_____

_____

_____

_____

_____

_____

_____

Chakra One Properties

Location .... In the perineum at the
base of the spine

Age of Resonance .... Conception to age 7

Shape .... Large cube

Glandular connection............... Cortex of the adrenal gland
(on the upper end of each
kidney in humans), which
secretes a number of
steroid hormones,
including the
corticosteroids cortisol and
corticosterone

Color .... Red

Musical note C

Type of music .... Drumming

Element .... Earth

Aspect of intelligence .... Administrative

Sensory experience................... Smell

Essential oils........................... Cinnamon, garlic,
sandalwood

Crystals .... Ruby, bloodstone, hematite

Aspects of the solar system ..... Earth, Saturn

Astrological association......... Capricorn

Metal .... Lead

Chakra One Properties

Earthly location..................... The Indian preserves and
their sacred lands; the
sacred lands of all
indigenous people.

Mythological animal .... White elephant with seven
trunks

Plant.. Sage

Qualities.................................... Patience, structure,
stability, security, the ability
to manifest dreams

Life issues .... To value the material as
sacred, to find trust in place
of despair, to persevere

Physical activities .... Yoga, movement of any
kind that activates the legs
and feet, any activity that is
grounding and physical and
demands presence

Spiritual activities .... Noticing the beauty and
perfection of the natural
world

Positive archetype..................... Mother

Negative archetype .... Victim

Angelic presence .... Archangel Michael, leader
of the heavenly armies
against the forces of evil

—Ambika Wauters

The Book of Chakras: Discover the Hidden Forces Within You

Healing Stones

Ruby, Bloodstone, Red Garnet, Red Sardonyx, Bixbite (Red Beryl), Ruby Aura Quartz, Red Spinel, Red Phantom Quartz, Red (Blood) Agate, Red Tiger's Eye, Red Aventurine, Black tourmaline, Hematite, Pyrite, Black and Snowflake Obsidian, Smoky Quartz

Ruby

Suggested Yoga Postures for Chakra One

English	Sanskrit
Grasshopper or Lotus	Shalabhasana
Wheel	Chakra Bandhasana
Bridge	Setu Bandhasana

Notes

_____

_____

_____

_____

_____

_____

_____

_____

_____

_____

_____

Meditation for Opening the Root Chakra

MUDRA FOR OPENING
ROOT CHAKRA

Review Muladhara's functions.

Sit comfortably with your spine straight and focus your attention on your perineum.

Form a circle with your forefingers and thumbs. Rest your hands on your knees with palms up.

Inhale deeply and as you exhale chant the mantra LAM three times. (Suggested musical note–C)

Repeat for 7 to 10 breaths.

Free form chant along with Baird Hersey's
Chakra One "Box of Red Earth"
Waking the Cobra: Vocal Meditations on the Chakras

Notes

_____

_____

_____

_____

_____

_____

_____

_____

_____

_____

_____

Short Affirmation

**I am safe
because the first chakra
of my energetic/spiritual body
is activated, open, and alive.**

*Memorize and repeat 3x in a row
at least 3x per day.*

Evolutionary Affirmation

I am a spiritual being having a human experience. I am a celestial being having a human experience. I know this is true because deep down I know myself as a spiritual being. I am inherently good.

I have purpose and value. I am capable of healing myself and others. I am safe, grounded, and centered because the first chakra of my energetic/ spiritual body is activated, open, and alive. My first chakra is balanced and spinning in its perfect direction for where I am right now, working toward my evolution, strengthening my celestial body, creating my Homo-luminous being.

*Read 1x per day while relaxed,
preferably after completing the meditations*

Guided Visualization

Sit in a comfortable position with your feet on the floor and your eyes closed. Imagine you are at the beach, sitting in a beach chair facing the ocean. The chair is low to the ground, and you can easily pick up sand and sift it through your fingers. The warm waves lap easily around your feet and legs, and at times gently and laughingly splash up onto your torso. Imagine that the ocean water is becoming filled with millions of tiny red rubies and garnets, sparkling, twinkling, glistening, and gleaming in the sun.

There are no sharp edges. They are all very smooth, soft, and delicate to the touch. The red jewels wash up on you, and you lazily pick up handfuls and release them into the wind. You feel perfectly centered, perfectly grounded, perfectly present. You feel safe, secure, comforted, and protected as you are surrounded with the magnificence of these jewels, understanding that you, too, are precious beyond compare. There will never be a moment in your life when you are not safe and cared for.

You trust that you are evolving.

You enjoy the process.

You enjoy your life.

Celestial Psychology® Principles: Chakra One

Human beings are spiritual beings or celestial beings having a physical experience; therefore, they are inherently good.

Human/spiritual/celestial beings have energy systems often called the energetic body.

The energetic/spiritual/ celestial body is capable of being strengthened or developed.

The energetic/spiritual/celestial body is the vehicle for change as well as the result of the change process itself.

Meditate on these principles.
Then journal with free association.

 Notes

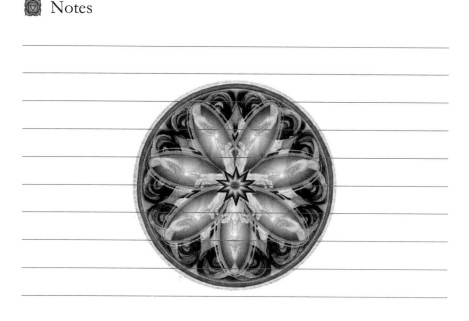

Journal Questions

After completing any of the exercises above, remain relaxed to answer the following questions.
Use free association.
Write your immediate response.
After answering "yes" or "no,"
add a brief explanation.
Don't overthink your answers.

Am I safe?

_____

_____

_____

_____

_____

Am I cared for?

_____

_____

_____

_____

_____

Am I secure?

_____

_____

_____

_____

_____

Journal Questions

Am I grounded?

_____

_____

_____

_____

_____

Do I take good care of myself?

_____

_____

_____

_____

_____

Do I nourish myself with support?

_____

_____

_____

_____

_____

Do I believe in myself?

_____

_____

_____

_____

_____

Journal Questions

Consider the ways in which the positive Archetype of The Mother may be influencing you:

"The Mother is a person, either male or female, who is nurturing, positive, and hopeful. Mothers encourage, acknowledge, and affirm our being through love, kindness, and absolute faith in the goodness of life. They make the dark moments bearable because they bring us hope of a positive outcome." —Ambika Wauters

_____

_____

_____

_____

_____

_____

_____

_____

_____

Consider the influence of the negative Archetype of The Victim:

"The victim is a person who, because of external circumstances, is unable to rally regenerative forces and go forward in life. Victims stay alive through the grace and generosity of other agencies and have little chance of renewing their connection with life as long as they remain dependent upon other to maintain life. They may be temporarily invalided, victims of terrifying circumstances, or completely uprooted from a life they have previously enjoyed." —Ambika Wauters

_____

_____

_____

_____

_____

_____

_____

_____

_____

Journal Questions

Ask yourself, "Is there something bothering me?" Write down the first things that come to mind.

_____

_____

_____

_____

_____

_____

_____

_____

_____

_____

_____

_____

Consider the ways the psychotherapeutic process and chakra one balancing will you help you improve your QOL and assist you on your evolutionary path.

_____

_____

_____

_____

_____

_____

_____

_____

_____

_____

_____

_____

Chakras – Energy System
Transformation Stations

Chakra Two

Svadhisthana
One's Own Place

Existential Therapy and Chakra Two

Although the second chakra, Svadhisthana, is most commonly associated with the right *to feel* and have pleasure, it also encompasses the right *to be* ourselves. *Sva* in Sanskrit means "self" and *dhisthana* means "its actual place" or "abode." Svadhisthana is "one's own place," which speaks to the core of our existence. Svadhisthana's function is to bridge the yin and yang, the male and female, the emotional and sensate aspects of consciousness, and the duality of self and higher consciousness. It is related to the element water, and it is located about one inch below the navel in the location of "tan tien" referenced in martial arts. It connects to the spinal column at lumbar vertebra number one and is associated with the lumbar-sacral and hypo-gastric plexuses. When our second chakra is balanced, it is impossible to be anything but authentic.

Existential therapies had their beginnings in the early 1900s. For this analysis, I am including these therapies in the first wave of psychoanalytical theory. Existential therapies were introduced with the work of Ludwig Binswanger (1881–1966) and Medard Boss (1903–1991). Both of these psychoanalysts were influenced by Freud. Existentialists are concerned with an individual's right to choose among varying degrees of existence, specifically how we exist in the world in relation to ourselves, nature, and others. Originally, existential psychoanalysts were more concerned with the orientation of existentialism than the actual development of a theoretical framework. It wasn't until the mid-fifties that Rollo May began to develop a coherent clinical approach. This approach was popularized in the eighties when Irving Yalom wrote Existential Psychotherapy. To the existentialists, "existence is best understood as being-in-the-world."[10] Serendipitously, this is Svadhisthana—one's own place.

Consciousness-raising is the art and practice of becoming *un*-self-conscious. Existential psychotherapists know that to be happy, we must drop the concerns that precipitate the formation of masks or false-selves that, in turn, perpetuate misery and suffering. They understand suffering is centered on four existential sources of angst: death, freedom and responsibility, isolation, and meaninglessness. In the introduction to his book, *Existential Psychotherapy*, Irvin D. Yalom writes, "The individual's confrontation with each of these facts of life constitutes the content of the existential dynamic conflict." Death, which we cannot escape, is the

> Consciousness-raising is the art and practice of becoming *un*-self-conscious.

ultimate anxiety producer. Spiritual, especially, religious beliefs combat this anxiety with after-life constructs. It is the process of making these constructs conscious that brings about the most authentic relief. Freedom to the existentialist "refers to the absence of external structure … [and] has a terrifying implication: it means that beneath us there is no ground—nothing, a void, an abyss." Existentialists say that taking responsibility for ourselves is the way out of angst.

On isolation, Yalom writes, "The existential conflict is thus the tension between our awareness of our absolute isolation and our wish for contact, for protection, our wish to be part of a larger whole." He also mentions this implies, "the individual is entirely responsible for—that is, is the author of—his or her own world, life design, choices, and actions."[11] Yalom identifies responsibility for oneself in general (let alone for creating one's own reality) as a major source of anxiety. The notion of the individual being the author of his or her own life is rampant in today's self-help literature. Blindly declaring "thoughts become things,"[12] has created undue angst for many seekers, until they understand there is much more to it than three simple words. And regarding meaninglessness, "each of us must construct our own meanings in life. Yet can a meaning of one's own creation be sturdy enough to bear one's life?"[13] Teaching clients to search deeply and honestly to uncover fears and to answer these basic fundamental questions about themselves and their existence is the crux of the existentialist's work. However, it is very difficult for most of us to answer these questions honestly.

"Since lying is the source of psychopathology, honesty is the solution for dissolving symptoms." The goal of existential psychotherapy is *authenticity*, so increasing consciousness is "...one of the critical processes through which people become aware of the aspects of the world and of themselves that have been closed off by lying."[14] Jean-Paul Sartre (1967), a French existentialist philosopher, wrote, "Man is nothing else but what he makes of himself. Such is the first principle of existentialism."[15]

Existentialists encourage clients to be authentic—to be whatever they want to be and to push themselves toward that goal. But first, they must experience themselves authentically and honestly, without any denial, and be able to express their feelings to the therapist without a mask or false self. A client's efforts to be authentic are enhanced when the therapist is able to authentically empathize with the client. Rollo May defined true empathy as "feeling into" the other. The psychotherapist *feels into* the client's personality until some state of identification is achieved. "[B]oth the client and the counselor merge into a common psychic entity."[16] Recall chakra two's ability to bridge or end duality. In existentialism the bridge is the empathic response between the therapist and the patient, and the result is an authentic understanding of where we stand—what *our own place is.*

The second chakra also addresses the rights *to feel* and *to want.* Svadhishthana's seed sound or mantra is "vam," its musical note is "D," its color is orange, and its element is water. The second chakra's functions are balancing the yin and yang, unifying polarities, and acknowledging humans as complicated and composed of light and dark thoughts and actions. Through the second chakra, existence can be experienced as the end of duality, the unification of all that causes existential angst with all that calms it. The second chakra focuses us on our emotions, creativity, sensuality, and sexuality, so blockages may result from imbalances and challenges in those areas of life. Repressed emotions can promote a build-up of fear, just as

In both existential therapy and chakra two activating, there is a search for and attraction toward opposites, inviting tremendous change, accepting new authentic thoughts, authentic experiences, and authentic modes of being.

excessive guilt can defeat joy. A prime example are the martyrs, who will separate themselves from pleasure, judge themselves, and believe they must be punished.

When working with chakra two within an existential framework, we are propelled toward completion of the whole self. We move toward the whole of existence, with no judgment or rejection. We are

"We humans appear to be meaning-seeking creatures who have had the misfortune of being thrown into a world devoid of intrinsic meaning. ...
The question of the meaning of life is, as the Buddha taught, is not edifying. One must immerse oneself into the river of life and let the question drift away."
—**Irvin D. Yalom**

encouraged to maintain safe and healthy boundaries and we expand our capacity for total expression. Thoughts are given more reign, moving beyond chakra one and mere psychoanalysis. In both existential therapy and chakra two activating, there is a search for and attraction toward opposites, inviting tremendous change, accepting new *authentic* thoughts, *authentic* experiences, and *authentic* modes of being.

Activating and balancing the second chakra combined with an existential focus has the potential for truly effective change. The second chakra unites the conscious with the unconscious, just as psychotherapy makes conscious what is unconscious. Looking squarely at death, freedom (free will), isolation, and meaninglessness is easier when the second chakra is activated. This work also accepts the shadow self—pieces of ourselves that we are not willing to admit to, or deem unacceptable, hideous, or too frightening to look at—as part of who we are in order to achieve balance and bring to consciousness the totality of our human existence. 🟤

In both existential therapy and chakra two activating, there is a search for and attraction toward opposites, inviting tremendous change, accepting new *authentic* thoughts, *authentic* experiences, and *authentic* modes of being.

Physiological Signs of Chakra Two Imbalance

The areas of the body governed by the second chakra are the lower intestines and abdomen, sexual and reproductive organs, prostate, ovaries, bladder and urinary system. Indicators of second chakra imbalance may be menstrual or menopausal difficulties; fibroids; lower back pain; knee, pelvis, or hip problems; or arthritis.

Psychological Signs of Chakra Two Imbalance

Signs of chakra two imbalance may include chronic (existential) anxiety/dread, a pervading sense of guilt (regarding lies or pretenses about self and reality), depression, sexual dysfunction (addiction or frigidity), deadened physical and emotional senses, imbalanced anima/animus, relationship issues (especially related to objectification of self or others), fear of being controlled by another, pattern of the prostitute archetype in relationships, creative blocks, or a denial or excess of pleasure.

Therapeutic Focus

Combine chakra balancing exercises with an existential focus by asking yourself questions such as the ones listed below. Focus on movement therapy, yoga, tai chi, martial arts, emotional release, inner child work, or 12-step programs.

◉ Notes

_____

_____

_____

_____

_____

_____

_____

_____

_____

_____

_____

Chakra Two Properties

Location .... Two inches below the navel and two inches into the pelvis

Age of Resonance 7–14

Shape .... Pyramid

Glandular connection .... Ovaries/testes

Color .... Orange

Musical note .... D

Type of music .... Latin music

Element .... Earth

Aspect of intelligence .... Sensation/pleasure

Sensory experience .... Taste

Essential oils........................... Jasmine, neroli, orange blossom

Crystals .... Carnelian, tiger's eye, onyx

Aspects of the solar system.... Jupiter

Astrological association.......... Cancer, Scorpio

Metal...................................... Tin

Chakra Two Properties

Earthly location ....Brazil

Mythological animal ....A hungry sea monster, waiting to be fed

Plant ....Jasmine

Qualities ....Well-being, sexuality, sensuality, pleasure, abundance

Life issues ....To know... you have enough... are enough; not to link self-worth with what you do or have... create healthy boundaries to protect your vital life force.

Physical activities...................Yoga, dance, swimming, walking

Spiritual activities ....Meditation, celibacy, fasting

Positive archetype ....Emperor/Empress

Negative archetype ....Martyr

Angelic presence.....................Archangel Metatron

—Ambika Wauters

The Book of Chakras: Discover the Hidden Forces Within You

Healing Stones

Carnelian, Rutilated Quartz, Orange Drusy Quartz, Fire Opal, Orange Hessonite Garnet, Agate, Tiger's Eye, Orange Calcite, Orange Jade, Orange-Brown Selenite, Orange Spinel, Tangerine Quartz, Orange Zircon

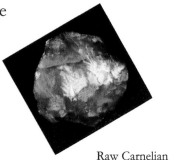

Raw Carnelian

Suggested Yoga Postures for Chakra Two

English	Sanskrit
Cobra	Bhujangasana
Twist	Ardha Matsyendrasana
Crocodile	Nakra-Kriyas

Notes

_____

_____

_____

_____

_____

_____

_____

_____

_____

_____

Meditation for Opening the Sacral Chakra

 Review Svadhisthana's functions.

 Sit comfortably with your spine straight and focus your attention on the area one-inch below your navel across to lumbar vertebra one.

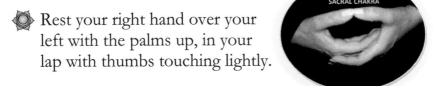
MUDRA FOR OPENING SACRAL CHAKRA

 Rest your right hand over your left with the palms up, in your lap with thumbs touching lightly.

 Inhale deeply and as you exhale chant the mantra VAM three times. (Suggested musical note–D)

 Repeat for 7 to 10 breaths.

> *Free form chant along with Baird Hersey's*
> *Chakra Two "Orange Crescent Moon"*
> *Waking the Cobra: Vocal Meditations on the Chakras*

 Notes

_____

_____

_____

_____

_____

_____

_____

_____

Short Affirmation

**I am a success
because the second chakra
of my energetic/spiritual body
is activated, open, and alive.**

*Memorize and repeat 3x in a row
at least 3x per day.*

Evolutionary Affirmation

I am capable of changing myself by raising my awareness to spirit. I have the freedom to transform my humanness into a divine self, a higher self, a celestial self. I use the power of my second chakra to achieve the success I need to change.

My second chakra allows me to achieve mastery over my humanness in all ways. My emotions and creativity blossom and flow. All my senses are activated. My second chakra is balanced and spinning in its perfect direction for where I am right now, working toward my evolution, strengthening my celestial body, creating my Homo-luminous being.

*Read 1x per day while relaxed,
preferably after completing the meditations.*

Guided Visualization

Sit in a comfortable position. Imagine holding a glass of freshly squeezed orange juice. Bring it to your lips and begin drinking it. Feel how cool and refreshing it is as it passes through your mouth, down your throat, and into your stomach and intestines. As it flows through you, it turns everything it touches a bright, rich orange.

Feel yourself radiating orange, and embrace the opening of your creativity and sensuality. All of your senses are opening. You feel vibrant, receptive, aware, and capable of navigating through your emotional landscape with ease. You are filled with juicy, jovial, life-filled orange.

You trust that you are evolving.

You enjoy the process.

You enjoy your life.

Celestial Psychology® Principles: Chakra Two

◉Human/spiritual/celestial beings are capable of change.

◉Consciousness-raising is the greatest vehicle for change.

◉Higher consciousness is often referred to as a power greater than oneself.

◉Consciousness plays a direct role in the effectiveness of energy as medicine.

Meditate on these principles.
Then journal with free association.

◉ Notes

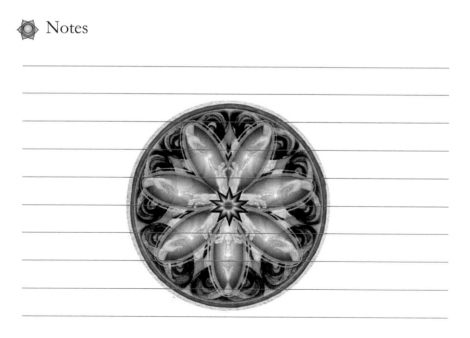

Journal Questions

After completing any of the exercises above, remain relaxed to answer the following questions.
Use free association.
Write your immediate response.
After answering "yes" or "no,"
add a brief explanation.
Don't overthink your answers.

Am I vital?

_____

_____

_____

_____

Am I flexible?

_____

_____

_____

_____

Am I satiated?

_____

_____

_____

_____

Journal Questions

◉Do I enjoy life?

_____
_____
_____
_____
_____

◉Do I accept pleasure?

_____
_____
_____
_____
_____

◉Do I keep good boundaries?

_____
_____
_____
_____
_____

◉Do I have meaning in my life?

_____
_____
_____
_____
_____

Journal Questions

◎ Consider the ways in which the positive archetype of The Emperor/Empress may be influencing you:

"The Emperor/Empress is a person who enjoys and respects the physical world. Emperors and Empresses love to have abundance, well-being, and a high degree of pleasure. They know they deserve to feel good about life and enjoy good food, comfort, and some luxury. They are not necessarily spiritual by nature but they do feel at home on the physical plane and enjoy the good life." —Ambika Wauters

_____

_____

_____

_____

_____

_____

_____

_____

◎ Consider the ways in which the negative archetype of The Martyr may be influencing you:

"Martyrs deprive themselves of the simple physical pleasures of life. At some basic level, they feel cheated of the goodness of life and punish themselves by forbidding themselves the warmth and comfort they long for. They are full of guilt and project this onto others, making them suffer too." —Ambika Wauters

_____

_____

_____

_____

_____

_____

_____

_____

_____

Journal Questions

◉ Consider how you are living your life. Are you taking full responsibility for yourself? How authentically are you living?

_____

_____

_____

_____

_____

_____

_____

_____

_____

_____

◉   ◉   ◉

◉ Consider ways an existential approach and chakra two balancing will help you improve your QOL and assist you on your evolutionary path.

_____

_____

_____

_____

_____

_____

_____

_____

_____

_____

_____

Gestalt Therapy and Chakra Three

The third chakra, Manipura, is considered the action chakra. It is located in the solar plexus area and is associated with the celiac plexus. It connects to the spine at the eighth thoracic vertebra and is understood to exist from the base of the ribcage to just above the navel. In Sanskrit, *mani* means "jewel" and *pura* means "place." Thus, Manipura is referred to as the "city of jewels" in the Hindu tradition. It is the chakra that governs our right *to act*. Yogananda[17] has claimed Maniupura to be the manger where the Christ consciousness can be born in each of us; however, it is mostly referred to as "the Warrior's chakra." Manipura is the chakra of physical and material power, and, when balanced, it promotes mastery and prompts our ability to manifest our hopes and dreams. Manipura is related to the element fire, and its nature is all about *will and raw energy*. Will and raw energy are also foundational to Gestalt therapy.

Gestalt therapy, considered in this analysis to be part of the second wave or force of psychoanalytical theory, was developed by Frederich (Fritz) Perls (1893–1970) in the 40s and became very popular in the 70s. Gestalt therapy continues to flourish under many umbrellas such as the practice of mindfulness. There are two basic tenets of Gestalt therapy: we must remain moment-centered, and we can only know ourselves in relation to others. Gestalt therapy has become known as a

> "Since maya is a mental world, a world of concepts, ideals, fantasies, and intellectual rehearsals, Perls says the way for us to become free from maya is to 'lose our mind and come to our senses.' This loss of mind is actually a radical change in consciousness from future-oriented thinking and theorizing to a present-oriented sensory awareness. At this phenomenological level of consciousness, we can experience with all of our senses the reality of ourselves and the world rather than just experiencing our theoretical or idealistic conceptions of how things are supposed to be. We can have the experience of *satori*, or waking up."
>
> **—Fritz Perls**

phenomenological approach to improving mental health. To master ourselves and our environment, and become more fully alive, we must clearly understand what is happening, and that involves using *objective* observation and description rather than *subjective* explanation.

Gestalts are the processes by which we continually bring completeness to what we need to survive and to make ourselves whole. This work is similar to the work discussed in chapters 3 and 4; however, there is another aspect that signals our spiral of consciousness-raising. This aspect is the liberation of an individual from the "maya," the world of the illusion, or the "phony, fantasy layer of existence. This is the desired goal of gestalt therapy."

"Since maya is a mental world, a world of concepts, ideals, fantasies, and intellectual rehearsals, Perls says the way for us to become free from maya is to 'lose our mind and come to our senses.' This loss of mind is actually a radical change in consciousness from future-oriented thinking and theorizing to a present-oriented sensory awareness. At this phenomenological level of consciousness, we can experience with all of our senses the reality of ourselves and the world rather than just experiencing our theoretical or idealistic conceptions of how things are supposed to be. We can have the experience of *satori*, or waking up."[18]

Of all the Western psychotherapeutic processes developed over the past century, Gestalt therapy is the most active for the client. For example, a Gestalt therapist might use the *empty chair* technique, directing the client to address an empty chair as if the object of the client's resentment is sitting in the chair. The therapist's work is to frustrate the client into action, encouraging them to yell, rant, and have a cathartic explosion to increase their awareness of phony games

Manipura is invested in initiative, making things happen, and, possibly more important, increasing self-esteem to the point of unflinching deserve-ability. Likewise, Gestalt therapy promotes letting go of the maya and bringing the individual to *satori*.

they are playing. Acting out polarities such as *Top Dog, Under Dog,* the client learns to come to a state of acceptance and experience their wholeness in the here-and-now. Processing suppressed anger is often a large part of the work, as the client's phony, phobic layers are revealed.

Fire is the element of the Manipura, and its color is yellow. Its seed sound is "ram," and its musical note is "E." As mentioned earlier, Manipura is the action chakra and, when balanced it is aligned with the goals of Gestalt therapy. When we are authentic and free from the maya, illusions of the egoic self, we are confident and have a pervading sense of psychic well-being. The third chakra and Gestalt therapy both focus on self-definition, with an emphasis on confronting negative boundaries and establishing or strengthening boundaries, as appropriate. Manipura is invested in initiative, making things happen, and, possibly more important, increasing self-esteem to the point of unflinching deserve-ability. Likewise, Gestalt therapy promotes letting go of the maya and bringing the individual to *satori*.

Combining third chakra work and gestalt techniques offers a way to break free from the world of illusion, the deceptive world the egoic mind desperately wants us to hang on to. We become free to act in ways that help us manifest our hopes and dreams. We are no longer insecure, anxious, mistrustful, or aggressive when our third chakra is balanced, and we have a true understanding of ourselves in relation to others in our lives. In other words, we are living our gestalt. We have a sense of purpose, and we pursue dreams that others may deem impossible. We realize that all choices belong to us. We are the creators of our own existence. We become powerful warriors; we use will, raw energy, a strong sense of balance, and healthy self-definition to protect our world and ourselves. 🌸

Gestalt Prayer
I do my thing and you do your thing. I am not in this world to live up to your expectations, And you are not in this world to live up to mine. You are you, and I am I, and if by chance we find each other, it's beautiful. If not, it can't be helped.
–Fritz Perls

Combining third chakra work and
gestalt techniques offers a way
to break free from the world of illusion,
the deceptive world
the egoic mind desperately
wants us to hang on to.

Physiological Signs of Chakra Three Imbalance

The third chakra governs the solar plexus, diaphragm, spleen, duodenum, stomach, pancreas, adrenals, gall bladder, liver, lower back, small intestine, skin, and sympathetic nervous system. Eating disorders, poor digestion, chronic fatigue, hypoglycemia, diabetes, hypertension, hernias, flatulence, addiction or attraction to stimulants or sedatives, and many symptoms of chakra two imbalance may indicate chakra three imbalance or blockage.

Psychological Signs of Chakra Three Imbalance

Unfounded feelings of powerlessness, shame, mistrust, aggression, and anxiety, and fears of rejection, criticism, looking foolish or having one's secrets discovered are symptoms of chakra three imbalance. Other indicators may be undue embarrassment over physical appearance; lack of confidence, self-esteem or self-respect; or imposter syndrome. Victimization, enmeshment in unhealthy situations, and the inability to trust one's intuition are major indicators of chakra three imbalance.

Therapeutic Focus

Combine chakra-balancing exercises with a gestalt focus by asking yourself questions such as the ones listed below. Focus on relaxation and stress management, healthy risk taking, martial arts, increased autonomy, and development of self and boundaries. Contemporary consciousness-raising practices considered spiritual in nature, such as mindfulness meditation, TM, yoga, t'ai chi and qigong have the same goals: self-acceptance and living in the here-and-now.

Notes

_____

_____

_____

_____

_____

_____

_____

_____

_____

_____

_____

Chakra Three Properties

Location .... Directly below the sternum and over the stomach

Age of Resonance 14–21

Shape .... Globe

Glandular connection .... Pancreas

Color .... Yellow

Musical note .... E

Type of music .... March

Element .... Fire

Aspect of intelligence .... Instinctual knowing

Sensory experience .... Vision

Essential oils........................... Lemon, grapefruit, juniper

Crystals .... Topaz, citrine, amber

Aspects of the solar system .... Mars and the Sun

Astrological association .... Aries, Leo

Metal...................................... Iron, gold

Chakra Three Properties

Earthly location ....United States of America

Mythological animal...............Lion

Plant.......................................Carnation

Qualities.................................Self-worth, self-esteem, confidence, personal power, freedom of choice

Life issues ....To develop a strong and resilient ego; to know you are worthy simply because you exist.

Physical activities ....Sports, competitive programs, qi gong, hiking, cycling

Spiritual activities ....Leadership programs, psychotherapy, amateur dramatics, appreciating solitude

Positive archetype...................Warrior

Negative archetype.................Servant

Angelic presence......................Archangel Uriel, regent of the Sun

—Ambika Wauters

The Book of Chakras: Discover the Hidden Forces Within You

Healing Stones

Golden Healer Quartz, Opal Aura Quartz, Sunshine Aura Quartz, Gold Sheen Obsidian, Citrine, Golden Calcite, Yellow Diamond, Yellow Herkimer, Yellow Topaz, Golden Tiger's Eye

Citrine

Suggested Yoga Postures for Chakra Three

English	Sanskrit
Bow	Dhanurasana
Seal	Vajroli Mudra
Cat	Bidalasana

Notes

_____

_____

_____

_____

_____

_____

_____

_____

_____

_____

Meditation for Opening the Solar Plexus

❂ Review Manipura's functions.

❂ Sit comfortably with your spine straight and focus your attention on the area of your navel to solar plexus and across to thoracic vertebra eight.

❂ With your fingers straight, touching at the top and pointing forward, form a V with your thumbs crossed right over left.

MUDRA FOR OPENING SOLAR PLEXUS CHAKRA

❂ Inhale deeply and as you exhale chant the mantra RAM three times. (Suggested musical note–E)

❂ Repeat for 7 to 10 breaths.

Free form chant along with Baird Hersey's
Chakra Three "Pyramid in Yellow"
Waking the Cobra: Vocal Meditations on the Chakras

❂Notes

_____

_____

_____

_____

_____

_____

_____

_____

Short Affirmation

**I am powerful
because the third chakra
of my energetic/spiritual body
is activated, open, and alive.**

*Memorize and repeat 3x in a row
at least 3x per day.*

Evolutionary Affirmation

I am driven to evolve. I work with the power of my third chakra to awaken my transformation to a homo-luminous being. All my actions are governed by my right to act in ways that produce the energy, vitality, and personal power necessary to complete this transformation. I choose only that which is good for  me and my boundaries keep me confident and strong in self-value. My third chakra is balanced and spinning in its perfect direction for where I am right now, working toward my evolution, strengthening my celestial body, creating my Homo luminous being.

*Read 1x per day while relaxed,
preferably after completing the meditations*

Guided Visualization

Sit in a comfortable position. Imagine you are in the middle of a field, lying down on your back in soft grass. Your arms and legs are spread comfortably, and your eyes are closed. Imagine the bright yellow sun exactly above you, touching every aspect of your body. Feel its warmth; feel its power; feel its total connection with your every cell.

Feel your body drinking up the bright yellow of the sun, coming in through your skin, pulsing through your blood stream, strengthening all your muscles and your bones. Bask in the brilliant yellow. Experience it filling you with strength, power, complete certainty, and personal brilliance. You trust that your third chakra is compelling you to actions that further your evolution!

You trust that you are evolving.

You enjoy the process.

You enjoy your life.

Celestial Psychology Principles: Chakra Three

 Human/spiritual/celestial beings are evolving from Homo sapiens to Homo-luminous beings.

Human/spiritual/celestial beings have evolutionary impulses that drive them to become fully actualized; therefore, becoming Homo luminous celestial beings is inevitable.

Meditate on these principles.
Then journal with free association.

Notes

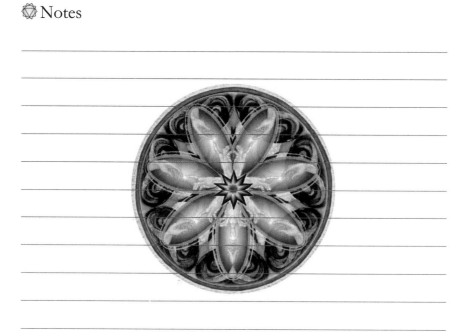

Journal Questions

*After completing any of the exercises above, remain
relaxed to answer the following questions.
Use free association.
Write your immediate response.
After answering "yes" or "no,"
add a brief explanation.
Don't overthink your answers.*

❀ Am I powerful?

_____

_____

_____

_____

_____

❀ Am I worthy?

_____

_____

_____

_____

_____

❀ Am I responsible?

_____

_____

_____

_____

Journal Questions

❂ Do I take appropriate action?

_____

_____

_____

_____

_____

❂ Do I accomplish what I set out to do?

_____

_____

_____

_____

_____

❂ Do I freely make my own good choices?

_____

_____

_____

_____

_____

❂ Do I fight the good fight?

_____

_____

_____

_____

Journal Questions

⬡ Consider the ways in which the positive archetype of The Warrior may be influencing you:

> "The warrior is an empowered person with a definitive sense of selfhood. Warriors know who they are in themselves and in relation to the world. Their sense of self is neither inflated nor weak. They have the inner strength and resilience to see their dreams materialize into reality and the stamina to meet physical and emotional challenges. They are able to fight the good fight for love, victory, and the glory of God."
>
> —Amika Wauters

_____

_____

_____

_____

_____

_____

_____

_____

⬡ Consider the ways in which the negative archetype of The Servant may be influencing you:

> "The servant is a person whose sense of personal identity is anchored in the external world, always seeking confirmation from others. Servants work hard for others' acknowledgment. They sabotage themselves by giving their power to others to define who they are and what they need to do. They lose energy trying to please others for the affirmation they are unable to give to themselves." —Amika Wauters

_____

_____

_____

_____

_____

_____

_____

_____

Journal Questions

❁ Consider someone you are resentful toward and using the action-based Gestalt of the empty-chair technique, i.e., go ahead and (talk or) write to the person(s) as if they are in the room with you.

_____
_____
_____
_____
_____
_____
_____
_____
_____
_____
_____

❁ ❁ ❁

❁ Consider the ways in which gestalts and chakra three balancing will you help you improve your QOL and assist you on your evolutionary path.

_____
_____
_____
_____
_____
_____
_____
_____
_____
_____
_____
_____
_____
_____

Chakras – Energy System
Transformation Stations

Chakra Four

Anahata
Unstruck, Unhurt

Interpersonal Psychology and Chakra Four

The fourth chakra, Anahata, is located in the heart area, also known as the cardiac plexus. This chakra connects to the spine at the first thoracic vertebra. Anahata focuses on healing and the love of self and others. Its full Sanskrit name, Anahata Nada, literally means "the eternal sound of the OM." This sound does not occur by any action, such as clapping one's hands, thus, it is "unstruck." It can only be heard when the heart chakra is opened during deep meditation. The more commonly accepted meaning of Anahata is "unhurt." The unhurt, or unbeaten, awakened heart chakra reaches into pure consciousness and hears the transcended *unstruck* sound of the cosmic OM.

Anahata resonates to the colors of green for healing and pink and rose for love. It is related to the element air, its sound is Yam, and the corresponding musical note is "E." As the centermost chakra, it circulates energy to the upper and lower chakras, while functioning to ensure balance and integration of mind and body, spirit and matter, and our inner and outer worlds. It focuses on healing and our ability to open our hearts to others while keeping healthy and clear boundaries. Anahata's right is the right *to love*. It is not about the physical pleasure of the second chakra, but heart-to-heart connections and relationships, including the most important one of all—our relationship to and our acceptance of ourselves. The fourth chakra also focuses on forgiveness, friends, pets, generosity, soul mates, and healthy giving. When Anahata is balanced, we stick up for our rights, express ourselves, resolve our feelings, and follow our own path. We no longer play psychological mind games, and we can enthusiastically say, "I'm OK, you're OK!"

> Anahata is about heart-to-heart connections and relationships, including the most important one of all—our relationship to and our acceptance of ourselves.

Interpersonal Psychotherapy (IPT) is classified here as part of the third wave or force of psychological theories. IPT began with the work of Harry Stack Sullivan and Adolph Meyer. They founded an interpersonal school for psychoanalysis in the 1950s based on the premise that psychopathology, especially depression, is not only a result of the individual's inadequate upbringing, but also is perpetuated by poor interpersonal skills, especially communication. IPT exists today as a twelve- to sixteen-visit brief therapeutic intervention.

Interpersonal Psychotherapies gained international fame with the work of two prominent psychiatrists, Eric Berne, MD (1910–1970) and Thomas A. Harris (1910–1995). Berne is the founder of Transactional Analysis (TA). His book, *Games People Play* (1964), has sold more than five million copies over the past forty years and has been translated into ten languages. It has enhanced the lives of millions of professionals and laypersons.

Using Berne's theory of Transactional Analysis, ego transactions are identified as coming from the ego states of the Parent, Child, or Adult. Each ego state functions as the *executive* at any particular time and each is broken down into more detailed substructures of the ego, for instance, the *Natural Child,* is spontaneous and creative and the *Adapted Child* is obedient. Ego states can be healthy or pathological. Because of TA, thousands of clients have learned to recognize and address unhealthy patterns (transactions), relieve confusion and stress, and improve behavioral habits. Typically, clients begin raising their

The cycle of giving and receiving joy and freedom is nurtured by the fourth chakra and by knowing that we are indeed OK.

consciousness through education, by reading the books of the TA authors. Once they have a grasp of the concepts, they begin individual therapy, progressing to group therapy. This is where they truly begin to bring TA into their everyday lives. Feedback from peers in the group is especially therapeutic as clients validate each other's interpretations of their transactions.

TA begins with a structural analysis where "...self-defeating transactions are made conscious, beginning with self-destructive games, leading to full awareness of the unhealthy life positions and life scripts that have been plaguing patients. With a curative increase in consciousness, clients are then able to choose which ego states to cathect at any particular time. With heightened awareness, they can also decide whether they will go on acting out tragic games, positions, and scripts or choose more constructive patterns of meeting their basic [needs]."[19]

Harris, an American psychiatrist and long-time friend of Berne, wrote two best-selling TA books, *I'm OK, You're OK* (1969) and *Staying*

OK (1974). These books, especially the former, are considered two of the most popular self-help books ever written. Harris cites four life positions as follows: (1) I'm Not OK, You're OK; (2) I'm Not OK, You're Not OK; (3) I'm OK, You're Not OK; and (4) I'm OK, You're OK, and then provides practical advice to decode transactions, communications, and relationships.

One of the greatest "OK" states achievable is that of forgiveness, another theme of the fourth chakra. Combining fourth chakra balancing with TA is a powerful way to promote self-forgiveness, self-acceptance, self-love, and the ability to see goodness in ourselves, which then allows us to see the goodness in others. The cycle of giving and receiving joy and freedom is nurtured by the fourth chakra and by knowing that we are indeed OK.

When balanced, the healthy fourth chakra's energy spreads upward and downward to the other chakras, providing them with love, comfort, and total acceptance. This is not to say the heart chakra opens to everything around it. It relies on the boundaries established by the third chakra to keep it safe from abuse and harm. Chakra balancing and TA invite us to bring to consciousness any codependent behaviors, and we are encouraged to discern healthy love from distortions of love or unhealthy behaviors done in the name of love ("I'm doing this because I love you.")

We improve our capacity for understanding, kindness, and tolerance when we do this work. It is nearly impossible to love others or ourselves without the sense of profound acceptance that comes from working with these concepts. Just as working the TA concepts can open the heart, achieving a balanced and integrated fourth chakra ensures there is nothing to say but, "I'm OK, You're OK." ✸

Just as working the TA concepts can open the heart, achieving a balanced and integrated fourth chakra ensures there is nothing to say but, "I'm OK, You're OK."

Physiological Signs of Chakra Four Imbalance

The areas of the body governed by the fourth chakra are the chest/breasts, rib cage, esophagus, shoulders, arms, lungs, heart, blood, circulatory system, immune system, and lymph glands. Physiological problems include any disorders of these areas, including inexplicable pain in the chest or between the shoulder blades, asthma, and breathing difficulties.

Psychological Signs of Chakra Four Imbalance

Signs of chakra four imbalance may include founded (actually happened) and unfounded (ego-scripted, exaggerated) grief over divorce, death, abandonment, or adultery; intolerance of others; rejection of self and others. Chakra four imbalance also manifests as challenges or conflicts with acceptance, love, loved ones, or friendships, and an inability to forgive or provide nurturance to self or others. Possible symptoms are loneliness, commitment phobia, emotional protection, jealousy, bitterness, anger, or hatred. Symptoms may also relate to personality disorders such as narcissism, codependence, possessiveness, lack of empathy, and a tendency to be critical, judgmental, or controlling.

Therapeutic Focus

Combine chakra-balancing exercises with TA by asking yourself questions such as the ones listed below. Focus on journaling, self-discovery, breathing, forgiveness, grief processing, inner child and Adult Child of Alcoholics (ACOA) work, codependency exploration, and working Twelve Steps of Co-dependents Anonymous (CoDA).

◉ Notes

_____

_____

_____

_____

_____

_____

_____

_____

_____

Chakra Four Properties

Location .... Middle of the chest

Age of Resonance 28–35

Shape .... Crescent moon

Glandular connection .... Thymus gland

Color .... Green for the heart
protector, pink or gold for
the heart itself

Musical note .... F

Type of music .... Choral

Element .... Air

Aspect of intelligence .... Remembering the good,
loving, and caring

Sensory experience .... Touch

Essential oils........................... Rose, carnation, lily of the
valley

Crystals .... Rose quartz, diamond,
peridot

Aspects of the solar system .... Mars and the Sun

Astrological association .... Libra and Taurus

Chakra Four Properties

Metal ....Copper and gold

Earthly location ....Spain

Mythological animal...............Deer

Plants ....Foxglove, rose, carnation, lily

Qualities..................................Unity, brotherhood/sisterhood, love, peace, purity, and innocence

Life issues ....To let love be the center of your life

Physical activities ....Yoga, massage, healing touch, walking, dancing

Spiritual activities ....Learning to love yourself first, then others, prayer, healing, singing, joyful endeavor

Positive archetype...................Lover

Negative archetype.................Actor/actress

Angelic presence.....................Archangel Raphael

—Ambika Wauters
The Book of Chakras: Discover the Hidden Forces Within You

Healing Stones

Emerald, Green Sapphire, Green Calcite, Green Tourmaline, Green Aventurine, Green Obsidian, Green Jasper, Malachite, Peridot, Actinolite, Apple Aura Quartz, Rhodochrosite, Rhodonite, Rose Quartz, Pink Sapphire, Pink Beryl, Pink Agate, Pink Petalite, Pink Fluorite, Pink Carnelian and Watermelon Tourmaline

Watermelon
Tourmaline

Suggested Yoga Postures for Chakra Four

English	Sanskrit
Camel	Ushtrasana
Fish	Matsyasana
Head to Knee	Janu Sirsana

Notes

_____

_____

_____

_____

_____

_____

_____

_____

Meditation for Opening the Heart Chakra

MUDRA FOR OPENING HEART CHAKRA

◈ Review Anahata's functions.

◈ Sit comfortably with your spine straight and focus your attention on the area of your heart across to thoracic vertebra one.

◈ Form a circle with your forefingers or middle fingers or both and thumbs. Rest your left hand palm up on your left knee. Raise your right hand up to the center of your breasts with palm angling slightly toward your heart.

◈ Inhale deeply and as you exhale chant the mantra YAM three times. (Suggested musical note–F)

◈ Repeat for 7 to 10 breaths.

Free form chant along with Baird Hersey's
Chakra Four "Golden Wind Emerald"
Waking the Cobra: Vocal Meditations on the Chakras

◈ Notes

_____

_____

_____

_____

_____

_____

_____

_____

Short Affirmation

**I am loving
because the fourth chakra
of my energetic/spiritual body
is activated, open and alive.**

*Memorize and repeat 3x in a row
at least 3x per day.*

Evolutionary Affirmation

I am open and loving to everyone and everything. I extend forgiveness to the best of my ability and I am working toward my own healing. I am connected to the universe. I am connected to the Divine Matrix. My fourth chakra makes this connection easily and freely by giving and receiving love. My fourth chakra is balanced and spinning in its perfect direction for where I am right now, working toward my evolution, strengthening my celestial body, creating my Homo-luminous being.

*Read 1x per day while relaxed,
preferably after completing the meditations*

Guided Visualization

Stand in a comfortable position with your arms out to the sides. Close your eyes and imagine you are a vine, a bright green, healthy, beautiful vine with your legs as the stems and your feet as the roots. As you stand, rotate your hands and arms very gently and slowly. Imagine that you are creating delicate tendrils from which blossom the softest and most beautiful tiny pink flowers. You may sway gently from side to side, imagining tendrils coming from your torso, your shoulders, your head.

Let your hands dance as you allow the pink flowers to bloom. You are completely covered in green and pink. You are immersed in love, inside and outside. You are extending this love out into the world for all to experience. You are in a state of active healing—alive, beautiful, peaceful, joyful. You trust that your fourth chakra is compelling you to be receptive to emotions that further your evolution.

You trust that you are evolving.

You enjoy the process.

You enjoy your life.

Celestial Psychology Principles: Chakra Four

◉ The outermost layers of the celestial body are the seat of consciousness and the intersection of the individual and the divine.

◉ Human/spiritual/celestial beings are connected to one another and the universe as a whole by what science defines as an energy grid, Field, or a Divine Matrix.

Meditate on these principles.
Then journal with free association.

◉ Notes

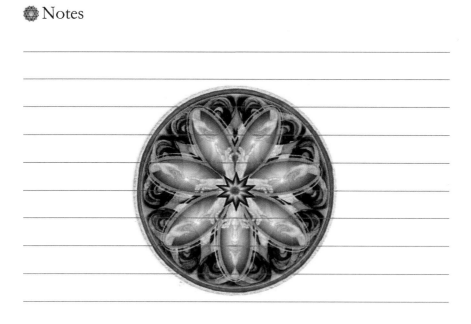

Journal Questions

*After completing any of the exercises above, remain
relaxed to answer the following questions.
Use free association.
Write your immediate response.
After answering "yes" or "no,"
add a brief explanation.
Don't overthink your answers.*

Am I OK?

_____

_____

_____

_____

_____

Am I loving and lovable?

_____

_____

_____

_____

_____

Am I balanced?

_____

_____

_____

_____

_____

Journal Questions

⚙ Do I forgive?

_____

_____

_____

_____

_____

⚙ Do I give and take?

_____

_____

_____

_____

_____

⚙ Do I easily accept myself and others?

_____

_____

_____

_____

_____

⚙ Do I say, "I'm OK, you're OK?"

_____

_____

_____

_____

_____

Journal Questions

⬡ Consider the ways in which the positive archetype of The Lover may be influencing you:

"The lover is a person whose ground of being is centered in the heart. They love unconditionally, and heal the tight, hard places in those they touch because they bring warmth and acceptance. They generate goodness and are genuinely embracing and kind. Their love is inclusive, uniting those on the outside. They share love with everyone. They know that to love is to live. Knowing the archetype changes your life for the good." —Ambika Wauters

_____

_____

_____

_____

_____

_____

_____

_____

⬡ Consider the ways in which the negative archetype of The Actor/Actress may be influencing you:

"This is a person whose love is conditional. They have expectations about the how and whom they can love. If someone falls outside of the realm of their conditions they withhold their love. They love in the limited way they have been loved, with judgment, and criticism for what doesn't fit into their framework. They love through imitation rather than true feeling. Their relationships often dry up because they have not developed a capacity to hold love in their hearts." —Ambika Wauters

_____

_____

_____

_____

_____

_____

_____

_____

Visuddha
Purification

Cognitive Therapies and Chakra Five

Chakra five, Visuddha in Sanskrit, is located in the throat area and connects with the spine at the third cervical vertebra, governing the nerves of the voice box, the pharyngeal plexus. The name Visuddha means "purification" or "purified"; *visha* means impurity, and *suddhi* means purify. It is related to the element ether, *akasha* in Sanskrit. It is the chakra of clear and constructive communication, accurate perception, and mental clarity. Visuddha focuses on our rights *to speak* and *to be heard*. It is associated with self-expression and our ability to assert ourselves and speak our truth. Chakra five relates to our ability to express anger and other emotions appropriately. It governs our ability to ask for what we need. With a balanced fifth chakra, we are better able to allow others into our lives and experience ourselves and others clearly. It is also associated with integrity, joy, and creativity. Visuddha also governs our management of personal space, and it is from here that we convey our personal integrity to the world. All we learn, create, or feel through our other chakras comes forth through our fifth chakra.

Because we communicate our truths (the truths we hold within us and the truths we all share collectively) through our fifth chakra, it must be balanced. We are not able to show or teach others who we are or express our completeness if Visuddha is blocked. People with blockages of the fifth chakra often say, "I'm just not creative." They may have a healthy second chakra, the home of creativity, but they are unable to express their creative gifts through their fifth chakra.

> With a balanced fifth chakra, we are better able to allow others into our lives and experience ourselves and others clearly.

Effectively purifying our belief systems and expressing ourselves for optimal mental health is what cognitive therapies are all about.

Cognitive therapies fuse well with studies of the fifth chakra because these therapies purify cognition, foster communication, and govern mental and perceptual clarity. Cognitive therapies, belonging to the third wave of psychological theory, are more intellectually oriented than behavioral approaches.

Albert Ellis (1913–2007) is renowned for being one of the most influential psychologists in history. He believed that irrational beliefs and unhealthy thoughts lead to unhealthy emotional states and negative behavior. He developed Rational Emotive Therapy (RET), and later Rational Emotive Behavior Therapy (REBT), revolutionizing passive psychoanalysis. In 1959, he founded The Institute for Rational Living, a non-profit training center for mental health professionals that still operates in New York City. REBT therapists assist clients to see themselves more clearly by exposing their irrational beliefs, much like the purifying function of chakra five.

REBT therapists use many different techniques. They may assign homework such as reading books written by REBT authors (who may or may not be their therapist at the time) and listening to "logic-driven audiotapes." Sometimes clients are required to listen to tapes of their own therapeutic sessions to help identify their "absolute and demanding" irrational beliefs. One of Ellis' favorite tasks was helping his patients overcome anxiety caused by not seeing oneself clearly, especially when it involves being too shy to speak or sing in public. He often used humor and singing to encourage them to get over their self-conscious and often self-defeating behaviors. "He wrote the song 'Perfect Rationality' (Ellis, 1991b) and required clients to sing it to the tune of Luigi Denza's 'Funiculi, Funicula.'"

Some think the world must have a right direction,
And so do I! And so do I!
Some think that, with the slightest imperfection,
They can't get by - and so do I!
For I, have to prove I'm superhuman,
And better far than people are!
To show I have miraculous acumen -
And always rate among the Great!
Perfect, perfect rationality
Is, of course, the only thing for me!
How can I ever think of being if I must live fallibly?
Rationality must be a perfect thing for me![20]

Ellis outlined his famous ABC's of RET: A represents Activating Events, B represents Beliefs we use to process Activating Events, and C represents Consequences of how we process A. The retort "RET is almost as easy as ABC" is still widely spoken in psychotherapeutic circles. Aaron Beck (1921–) coined different terms for cognitive therapy, but his premise is similar to Ellis'.

"…helping clients to *become conscious* [italics added] of maladaptive cognitions, to recognize the disruptive impact of such cognitions, and to replace them with more appropriate and adaptive thought patterns."[21]

Beck became famous for the phrases "maladaptive cognitions, dysfunctional attitudes, and depressogenic assumptions," but his true claim to fame is his Depression Inventory. This extremely effective Likert scale[22] questionnaire not only quantifies the depth of depression, but also provides a road map into the maladaptive cognitions, dysfunctional attitudes, and depressogenic assumptions that are at play in the psyche.

Typically, clinicians read the inventory questions aloud and invite discussion. For example, question 9 reads: Suicidal Thoughts or Wishes: (0) I do not have any thoughts of killing myself, (1) I have thoughts of killing myself, but I would not carry them out, (2) I would like to kill myself, (3) I would kill myself, if I had the chance. Or question 21: Loss of Interest in Sex: (0) I have not noticed any recent change in my interest in sex, (1) I am less interested in sex than I used to be, (2) I am much less interested in sex now, (3) I have lost interest

Communication is a skill that you can learn.
It's like riding a bicycle or typing.
If you're willing to work at it,
You can rapidly improve the quality of every part of your life.
—**Brian Tracy, Life Coach**

in sex completely. Such questions can provoke a wide variety of responses and the potential for lively discourse, all of which helps the therapist to establish the client's levels of cognitive impairment or deficits. Within two sessions, a therapist using this tool can determine an appropriate level of care for the client.

With cognitive therapies, once we have processed (or *purified*) our cognitions, the best tool for expressing ourselves is the assertiveness formula. We need to be able to say, "This is how I see it;" "This is how it makes me feel;" and "This is what I need." This formula appears simple, yet it is extremely difficult to utilize, especially when we are either habitually passive or aggressive. A healthy fifth chakra makes this tool much easier to incorporate into our communications.

The themes of *purification* and *enhanced communication* of the fifth chakra are vitally important in understanding ourselves, how we think, and how we react in concert with others. Good communication is not only about our own voice, it's also about our ability to listen well to others. Cognitive therapies and chakra five activating and balancing techniques help us recognize the voices of our internal conversations. We become adept at recognizing our thought patterns, e.g., what we tell ourselves and whether our thoughts are rational or irrational, appropriate or dysfunctional. We learn to discern whether we are being critical, judgmental, or untruthful. We develop the ability to transform anger, grief, and fear into healthy emotions and positive, appropriate actions. This combination of tools, this transformation station of *purification* and cognitive restructuring, provides the impetus to healthy self-expression. It gives us the ability to assertively move forward, and to speak our truths with clarity, confidence, and integrity. We say, "Yes!" to change. ✽

> Cognitive therapies and chakra five activating and balancing techniques help us recognize the voices of our internal conversations. We become adept at recognizing our thought patterns, e.g., what we tell ourselves and whether our thoughts are rational or irrational, appropriate or dysfunctional.

This combination of tools – this transformation station of *purification* and cognitive restructuring, provides the impetus to healthy self-expression. It gives us the ability to assertively move forward, and to speak our truths with clarity, confidence, and integrity.
We say, "Yes!" to change.

Physiological Signs of Chakra Five Imbalance

The fifth chakra governs the thyroid, parathyroid, hypothalamus, vocal cords, lower neck, jaw, throat, trachea, esophagus, mouth, teeth, and ears, although some include ears in the sixth chakra. Symptoms of fifth-chakra imbalance include diseases associated with these areas of the body as well as tone-deafness, or a weak or overbearing voice. Symptoms such as headaches, shortness of breath, fatigue, dizziness, weakness, gum disorders, tightness of the jaw, chronic cough or hoarseness, and heartburn (especially from excessive eating and drinking to keep the throat busy), may be associated with an undiagnosed disorder of a fifth-chakra body area .

Psychological Signs of Chakra Five Imbalance

Psychological symptoms of fifth-chakra imbalance include problems with open, honest communication such as fears of losing one's voice, not being heard, or having to speak up. Inability to discern one's truths or inability to trust others because of cognitive deficiencies, listening skills deficits, specifically, poor comprehension of what others are communicating, is another symptom. The inability to assert oneself truthfully in order to get one's needs met is probably the most common symptom. Inability to communicate well with writing or artistic ventures, especially writer's block for professional writers, is also a very telling symptom. Also noteworthy are behaving either overly shy or interruptive; engaging in gossip; and engaging in negative or toxic behaviors, such as, bad-mouthing, pitting people against each other, manipulating, or controlling.

Therapeutic Focus

Combine chakra-balancing exercises with cognitive therapy by asking yourself questions such as the ones listed below. Focus on releasing one's true voice, singing, chanting, yodeling, storytelling, journaling, silence, automatic writing, and letter writing (especially the get-it-all-out ones we don't intend to send). Improve communication skills and develop vulnerability in sharing oneself. Develop a sense of humor!

Notes

_____

_____

_____

_____

_____

_____

_____

_____

_____

Chakra Five Properties

Location ....The internal and external throat

Age of Resonance 35–42

Shape.....................................An inverted pyramid, suspended around the jaw and pointing down toward the heart

Glandular connection ....Thyroid and parathyroid glands

Color.....................................Turquoise

Musical note...........................G

Type of music ....Opera

Element..................................The ethers, in which all things are contained

Aspect of intelligence ....Will and expression

Sensory experience ....Hearing

Essential oils ....Blue chamomile, gardenia, ylang ylang

Crystals..................................Turquoise, blue agate, aquamarine

Aspects of the solar system.....Mercury

Astrological association..........Gemini, Virgo

Chakra Five Properties

Metal.. Copper and gold

Earthly location .... Italy

Mythological animal .... Sparrow hawk

Plants .... Gardenia

Qualities .... Will, communication, creativity

Life issues.............................. To harness your will, to express your highest truth, to live creatively

Physical activities .... Alexander technique, yoga, osteopathic alignment of the spine, cranio-sacral therapy, expressive theater and dance, qi gong, tai chi

Spiritual activities .... Chanting, silent retreats, fasting, yoga, prayer, meditation, singing, keeping a journal, public speaking, bearing witness

Positive archetype .... Communicator

Negative archetype .... Silent child

Angelic presence .... Archangel Gabriel, who brings the word of God

—Ambika Wauters

The Book of Chakras: Discover the Hidden Forces Within You

Healing Stones

Turquoise, Aquamarine, Larimar, Blue
Topaz, Blue Tourmaline (Indicolite),
Aqua Aura Quartz, Siberian Blue
Quartz, Angelite, Andean Blue
Opal, Kyanite, Blue Lace Agate,
Blue Obsidian, Blue Jasper, Blue
Spinel, Sodalite

Aqua Aura

Suggested Yoga Postures for Chakra Five

English	Sanskrit
Shoulder Stand	Sarvangasana
Plough	Halasana
Fish	Matsayana

Notes

_____

_____

_____

_____

_____

_____

_____

_____

_____

_____

Meditation for Opening the Throat Chakra

🌸 Review Visuddha's functions.

🌸 Sit comfortably with your spine straight and focus your attention on the area of the base of your throat across to cervical vertebra three.

MUDRA FOR OPENING THROAT CHAKRA

🌸 Form a circle with your thumbs touching and the rest of your fingers crossed and loosely cupped. Raise your hands in front of your throat, solar plexus, or rest them on your lap.

🌸 Inhale deeply and as you exhale chant the mantra HAM three times. (Suggested musical note–G)

🌸 Repeat for 7 to 10 breaths.

Free form chant along with Baird Hersey's
Chakra Five "Spinning Blue Sphere"
Waking the Cobra: Vocal Meditations on the Chakras

🌸 Notes

_____

_____

_____

_____

_____

_____

_____

_____

Short Affirmation

**I am communicative
because the fifth chakra
of my energetic/spiritual body
is activated, open, and alive.**

*Memorize and repeat 3x in a row
at least 3x per day.*

Evolutionary Affirmation

I love to do Holy Work. I love to do Holy Work for myself and for others. I love to do all that raises consciousness, for my-Self and for others. I communicate clearly, logically and truthfully about all areas of my life. I am assertive and effective. I speak truths that raise the consciousness of others, as well as my own. I use my voice to assist the evolution of mankind. I listen closely, carefully, and deeply. My fifth chakra is balanced and spinning in its perfect direction for where I am right now, working toward my evolution, strengthening my celestial body, creating my Homo luminous being.

*Read 1x per day while relaxed,
preferably after completing the meditations*

Guided Visualization

Sit in a comfortable position. Imagine that you are standing in front of a door that leads to the outdoors. Take a few deep breaths and open the door to begin your day. You are greeted by the most beautiful blue sky you have ever seen.

Fluffy white clouds float by gently. Blue birds and blue jays fly by joyfully. They land on the tree branches near you and on the ground by your feet. You can see a beautiful and sparkling blue body of water off in the distance.

You breathe deeply, closing your eyes and imagining the blue entering your nose and nestling in your throat chakra. It is fresh and invigorating. You feel clear and free. You are ready to listen deeply and speak clearly in all you do today. Your truth is set free in a healthy expression of who you really are. You trust that your fifth chakra is compelling you to express all that furthers your evolution.

You trust that you are evolving.

You enjoy the process.

You enjoy your life.

Celestial Psychology Principles: Chakra Five

- The development of consciousness is referred to as consciousness-raising. In Celestial Psychology® it is referred to as "Holy Work."

- Consciousness-raising aka Holy Work is integral to Celestial Psychology®.

- Celestial Psychology® is the "Holy Work" of evolving from Homo sapiens to Homo luminous beings.

- "Holy Work" is the responsibility of the individual; however, when being performed or practiced, its efficacy is enhanced by the individual's focus on divine or celestial forces, which are omniscient and omnipresent.

*Meditate on these principles.
Then journal with free association.*

- Notes

Journal Questions

After completing any of the exercises above, remain relaxed to answer the following questions.
Use free association.
Write your immediate response.
After answering "yes" or "no,"
add a brief explanation.
Don't overthink your answers.

Am I assertive?

_____

_____

_____

_____

_____

Am I honest?

_____

_____

_____

_____

_____

Am I a good listener?

_____

_____

_____

_____

_____

Journal Questions

🔘 Do I honor my truth?

_____
_____
_____
_____

🔘 Do I behave with integrity?

_____
_____
_____
_____

🔘 Do I say what I mean, and mean what I say?

_____
_____
_____
_____

🔘 Do I speak (and sing) clearly and confidently?

_____
_____
_____
_____

Journal Questions

⚙ Consider the ways in which the positive archetype of The Communicator may be influencing you:

> "This is a person who lives from personal integrity. Communicators tell the truth to the best of their ability. They are skilled in putting words to their feelings and they are able to stand up for what they believe. They say no when they need to and their word can be trusted."

—**Ambika Wauters**

_____

_____

_____

_____

_____

_____

_____

_____

_____

⚙ Consider the ways in which the negative archetype of The Silent Child may be influencing you:

> "This is a person who has suppressed expressiveness because of fear or shame. These people hide their feelings and are not connected to their higher truth. They say yes when they mean no."

—**Ambika Wauters**

_____

_____

_____

_____

_____

_____

_____

_____

_____

Journal Questions

Write about a time in your life when you used your voice to overcome shyness, insecurity, or passivity.

_____

_____

_____

_____

_____

_____

_____

_____

_____

_____

_____

_____

_____

_____

_____

_____

Consider the ways in which cognitive therapies and chakra five balancing will you help you improve your QOL and assist you on your evolutionary path.

_____

_____

_____

_____

_____

_____

_____

_____

_____

_____

_____

_____

_____

_____

_____

Chakras – Energy System
Transformation Stations

Chakra Six

Ajna
To Perceive or To Command

Humanistic Theory, Transpersonal Psychology, and Chakra Six

The sixth chakra is located between our eyebrows in the space called our "third eye." Its point of contact on the spine is the first cervical vertebra, and it is associated with the nasociliary plexus. Its center (depicted as a white bead) is near the pineal and pituitary glands, and its radius includes the medulla oblongata and the skull's interior. Both the sixth chakra and the pineal gland are often referred to as the third eye. Because the third eye's main function is to see inward and outward, its rights are *to see* and *to be seen*. In Sanskrit, the name *Ajna* means "to command," and acting as a command center is Anja's main function. Considered the chakra of wisdom, vision, and knowledge, it also functions as a perception center, and the name Ajna has grown to mean "to perceive." Ajna encompasses our ability to understand the vastness of all things and the ways in which the universe works—past, present, and future. The sixth chakra, whose element is light or energy, as in electrical or telepathic, relates to the psychic faculty of inner seeing, insight, and extra-sensory perception.

Ajna opens us to the beauty of the inner world, the symbolic realm of archetypes and dreams, and the awakening of a guiding vision. Memory, higher intuition, reasoning, and rational deductive thought—all are constituents of the sixth chakra. It correlates perfectly to the transcendent qualities of Humanistic and Transpersonal theories, now classified as the fourth wave of psychological theory. Abraham H. Maslow (1908–1970) was the founder of Humanistic Psychology. Humanistic therapies are typically considered the third wave of psychology. However, I am placing them alongside the transpersonal therapies of the fourth wave of psychological theory because they closely resemble each other and were developed by the same group of colleagues.

Maslow is best known for creating the Hierarchy of Needs theory, famously depicted in the shape of a pyramid. In Maslow's opinion, once we are self-actualized and at the top of the pyramid, we are capable of having peak experiences. A review of peak experiences detailed in his book, *Religions, Values, and Peak-Experiences (1964)*, reveals an extraordinary connection to spirituality and consciousness-raising. He defined 25 qualities of peak experiences that were typically thought to be only religious, but he saw they cured "chronic anxiety neurosis ... and strong obsessive thoughts of suicide." The first characteristic happens when one experiences the following: "the whole universe is perceived as an integrated and unified whole." In the third characteristic he writes, "The peak-experience seems to lift us to greater than normal heights so that we can see and perceive in a higher than usual way." Peak experiences are highly valuable—intrinsic to mental and emotional health, giving life meaning, and contributing to high-level wellness.[23]

Maslow's work foreshadowed the New Age concept of the ego as *the egoic mind*, in which the ego or the egoic mind is not limited to the classical Freudian interpretation. Rather, the ego is now used in a broader more encompassing way to describe all of consciousness that is not identified with the essential self.[24] Maslow described the self-actualized individual as "relatively ego-transcending, self-forgetful, egoless, unselfish." He believed that when we live in a sacred world where there is no time, no position, no conflict, and no anxiety, the "heaven that emerges from the peak experiences is one which exists all the time all around us, always available to step into for a little while at least."[25] It is here that we experience wonder, gratitude, awe, reverence, honesty, spontaneity, love, and our divinity. Just as with the sixth chakra, Ajna.

"My thesis is that new developments in psychology are forcing a profound change in our philosophy of science, a change so extensive that we may be able to accept the basic religious [spiritual] questions as a proper part of the jurisdiction of science, once science is broadened and redefined."[26]

—Abraham Maslow

The "new developments" of which Maslow spoke are embodied in the field of transpersonal psychology. Transpersonal psychology has been popularized as the fourth wave of psychology, and will remain so within the context of this framework.

Maslow, along with other transpersonal psychologists, such as Roberto Assagioli (1988–1974), Anthony Sutich (1907–1976), and Stanislav Grof, M.D., Ph.D. (1931–), set out to integrate ancient wisdom from mystical and esoteric traditions around the world with contemporary Western psychology. Their pioneering work led to the establishment of the Association for Transpersonal Psychology in 1971. Grof, the founding and current president of the International Transpersonal Association and professor of psychology has taken the peak experience to its idiomatically literal meaning with his research, writings, and teachings about LSD. The typical LSD or hallucinogenic "trip" increases in intensity from the moment of ingestion to its climax or *peak* and then intensity subsides until the substance wears off. His research, having been both experiential and didactic, lends itself to accuracy and evidence of altered states of reality that are often experienced when working with the energies of chakra six. Grofdefines non-ordinary states of consciousness as "holotropic."

"This composite word literally means 'oriented toward wholeness' or 'moving in the direction of wholeness' (from the Greek *holos*, whole, and *trepein*, moving toward or in the direction of something). This term suggests that in our everyday state of consciousness we identify with only a small fraction of who we really are. In holotropic states of consciousness, we can transcend the narrow boundaries of the body ego and reclaim our full identity. We can experientially identify with anything that is part of creation and even with the creative principle itself."[27]

Hallucinogenic drugs are not necessary to achieve altered states of mind. Holotropic or non-ordinary states of consciousness occur *naturally* with meditation, especially sixth chakra balancing. A well-known story portrayed in the book, *Miracle of Love*, by Ram Dass (1995), formerly known as Dr. Richard Alpert, tells of Alpert's travel to India to learn meditation and become enlightened.

Perhaps because of his acquaintance with Timothy Leary and Stanislov Grof, Alpert brought a small stash of LSD along for research and to help him achieve nirvana. The Maharajji, upon learning of Alpert's LSD, asked him to hand it over. Reluctantly, Alpert did so and was stunned when the guru downed the entire handful. Alpert was more stunned that the Maharajji was completely unaffected by the drug. The guru wanted Alpert to witness truths about maya and illusion: with meditation and God-consciousness, the Maharajji's brain was already *there*.

The sixth chakra's influence is quite extensive in that it works with both the left and right brain hemispheres to balance them and bring them to unification. Sometimes described

And you can fly
High as a kite if you want to
Faster than light if you want to
Speeding through the universe
Thinking is the best way to travel.
—The Moody Blues

as our hard drive or quality-control center, the sixth chakra broadens our understanding of the big picture, giving us far-sightedness and the ability to clearly see the truth. It also introduces us to the world of symbols, patterns, insights, interpretations, and *Aha!* moments. Similar to Maslow's definitions of peak experiences, this work enhances our ability to see and "step into heaven- if only for a little while."

When the sixth chakra is blocked, we choose to see only with our physical senses. We are afraid of intuition, dreams, imagination, or anything we perceive as spiritual power or prowess. We believe cultural fears and superstitions to be real-world. We view life in general and our existence in particular as awful, negative, and everyone else's fault. We criticize, judge, and overly intellectualize; we are small-minded and obsessive, critical, and judgmental.

The work of balancing the sixth chakra and accessing higher consciousness with the humanistic and transpersonal psychologies *is* the same work. When our sixth chakra is open and healthy, we see life as it is—glorious, unified, and on a hopeful and upward evolutionary trajectory. When we are self-actualized and have transcended the ego, we see life as the spiritual adventure that it is. We untie the karmic knots, the negative patterns of our own pasts, lifetimes, and ancestry. We see through the darkness of illusions and non-truths in ourselves and others. We develop inner knowing, trust in our own innate wisdom, and acknowledge we are capable of co-creating our own reality with a strong, clear mind.

> **The work of balancing the sixth chakra and accessing higher consciousness with the humanistic and transpersonal psychologies *is* the same work. When our sixth chakra is open and healthy, we see life as it is— glorious, unified, and on a hopeful and upward evolutionary trajectory. When we are self-actualized and have transcended the ego, we see life as the spiritual adventure that it is.**

Physiological Signs of Chakra Six Imbalance

The areas of the body governed by the sixth chakra are head, eyes, all senses, brain (especially the frontal lobes), nervous system, pituitary, and pineal glands. Some obvious symptoms of imbalance include all diseases associated with these areas as well as persistent headaches or migraines, insomnia, nightmares, hallucinations, delusions, and memory problems. Not so obvious indications of imbalance are addictions, anxiety, depression, deficient immune system, chronic sinusitis, and an inability to recall one's dreams or visualize the future.

Psychological Signs of Chakra Six Imbalance

Psychological signs of sixth chakra imbalance relate to lack of trust or belief in essential self and all things that are intuitive, psychic, or non-material. Symptoms can manifest as confusion (especially about life in general), defensiveness, projection, or unwillingness to look at truth in relation to self. Inability to deal with the dark side of the unconscious or one's shadow and being judgmental or superstitious are signs of imbalance, as are obsessions, delusions, concentration issues, detachment challenges, dream life difficulties, and indecisiveness. A minimal imagination or an overactive intellect that rules heart and gut may signal a sixth-chakra imbalance.

Therapeutic Focus

Combine chakra-balancing exercises with transpersonal exercises by asking yourself questions such as the ones listed below. Focus on memory techniques, creative art therapy, guided visualizations, dream analysis, past life work, Transcendental Meditation (TM), and mindfulness. Practice observing and releasing the negative egoic mind, illusions, and denial in order to integrate the Self.

 Notes

_____

_____

_____

_____

_____

_____

_____

_____

_____

_____

_____

_____

_____

Chakra Six Properties

Location	Between the eyebrows
Age of resonance	35-42
Shape	Five pointed star
Glandular Connection	Pituitary gland
Color	Indigo
Musical note	A
Type of Music	Classical, especially Mozart sonatas
Element	The Cosmos
Aspect of intelligence	Control and wisdom
Sensory experience	Mindful knowing/intuition
Essential oils	Camphor, sweet pea, heliotrope
Crystals	Sapphire, tanzanite, lapis lazuli
Aspects of the Solar System	The Moon
Astrological associations	Sagittarius, Pisces
Metal	Silver
Earthly Locations	Peru and the Rocky Mountains
Mythological animal	Hawk
Plant	Almond blossom

Chakra Six Properties

Life issues .... To focus your intelligence; to know who and what are for your highest good and greatest joy; to distill wisdom from your life experiences, both good and difficult; to choose life, health, joy and fulfillment in every aspect of your life

Physical activities .... Yoga, tai chi, qi gong, Bates eye exercises

Spiritual activities .... Thinking clearly about your life, reading or viewing uplifting and positive books or films, reflection, contemplation, meditation, and creative use of your imagination to visualize the life you say you want

Positive archetype .... Wise person or elder

Negative archetype .... Intellectual

Angelic presence .... The Shekhinah, better known as the feminine face of God

—Ambika Wauters
Book of Chakras: Discover the Hidden Forces Within You

Healing Stones

Indigo & Royal Blue Sapphire,
Azurite, Lapis Lazuli, Blue
Agate, Blue Jade, Blue Halite,
Blue Howlite, Blue
Aventurine, Blue Fluorite,
Iolite, Scapolite, Blue Opal
(Girasol), Celestite (Celestine)

Celestite

Suggested Yoga Postures for Chakra Six

English	Sanskrit
Seating Posture	Yoga Mudra
Fish	Matsayana
Shoulder Stand	Sarvangasana

Notes

_____

_____

_____

_____

_____

_____

_____

_____

_____

_____

Meditation for Opening the Eye Chakra

MUDRA FOR OPENING THIRD EYE CHAKRA

- Review Ajna's functions.

- Sit comfortably with your spine straight and focus your attention on the area of your third eye, beginning slightly above the point between the eyebrows across to cervical vertebra one, encompassing the skull's interior.

- Form a heart with your thumbs touching at the tips and your forefingers, ring and pinky fingers touching at the second phalanges. Raise your middle fingers to form a crown. Raise your hands in front of your third eye, solar plexus, or rest them on your lap.

- Inhale deeply and as you exhale chant the mantra OM three times. (Suggested musical note–A)

- Repeat for 7 to 10 breaths.

Free form chant along with Baird Hersey's
Chakra Six "Through the Violet Eye"
Waking the Cobra: Vocal Meditations on the Chakras

- Notes

_____

_____

_____

_____

_____

_____

_____

Short Affirmation

**I am creative
because the sixth chakra
of my energetic/spiritual body
is activated, open, and alive.**

*Memorize and repeat 3x in a row
at least 3x per day.*

Evolutionary Affirmation

I co-create with the divine. I co-create my reality. The more Holy Work I do, the more I know the divine. I am gaining insight into what my spiritual, divine, celestial being will look, think like, and behave like. I create a miraculous life. I create miracles for myself and others. I can see with my mind's eye all that is divine.

My mind is sharp, powerful, creative, and brilliant.

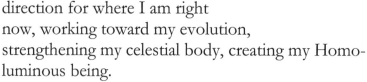

I know all things, because my mind is one with the divine. My sixth chakra is balanced and spinning in its perfect direction for where I am right now, working toward my evolution, strengthening my celestial body, creating my Homo-luminous being.

*Read 1x per day while relaxed,
preferably after completing the meditations.*

Guided Visualization

Sit in a comfortable position. Place your hands in prayer position, and lift them up until your thumbs are touching your third eye. Imagine your mind being flooded with an inky indigo blue. There are brilliant points of light in the indigo, like stars in a midnight sky. The stars are exquisitely positioned on your night canvas. Your vision intensifies and you understand that each star is a piece of yourself.

Some may be your ancestors or guardians watching over you. Some may be parts of your life journey—both its memories and goals. Some are friends and family—past, present, and future. Spend a moment contemplating these stars. Understand their messages for you, for your sixth chakra has opened and your intuition and clarity are impeccable. Your journey becomes clear. You trust that your sixth chakra is compelling you to know all that will further your evolution.

You trust that you are evolving.

You enjoy the process.

You enjoy your life.

Celestial Psychology Principles: Chakra Six

Human/spiritual/celestial beings are co-creators with divine or celestial forces. They co-create reality, and the more developed their celestial bodies become, the more efficacious and miraculous their creations may become.

Human/spiritual/celestial beings develop their understanding of the divine best by finding their own path(s), bypassing dogmatic or bureaucratic ideologies.

Psychotherapy is the ultimate form of healing because all healing comes from the mind.

Meditate on these principles.
Then journal with free association.

Notes

Journal Questions

After completing any of the exercises above, remain
relaxed to answer the following questions.
Use free association.
Write your immediate response.
After answering "yes" or "no,"
add a brief explanation.
Don't overthink your answers.

Am I intuitive?

_____

_____

_____

_____

_____

Am I creative?

_____

_____

_____

_____

_____

Am I insightful?

_____

_____

_____

_____

_____

Journal Questions

Do I know myself in this life-time and past life-times?

_____

_____

_____

_____

_____

Do I trust what I see and know?

_____

_____

_____

_____

Do I visualize my future?

_____

_____

_____

_____

Do I use my wise mind?

_____

_____

_____

_____

Journal Questions

Consider the ways in which the positive archetype of The Wise Person may be influencing your life:

> "This is a person who has cultivated wisdom, which the Bible says is more valuable than gold. Wise people offer the best of their life experience to assist others along the path of life. They encourage spiritual pursuits and physical adventures as well as guiding us in making optimally wholesome choices for ourselves. Wise people live by universal principles and trust in a higher source to guide them through the peaks and valleys of life, and with good fortune they assist us in leading ours." —Ambika Wauters

Consider the ways in which the negative archetype of The Intellectual may be influencing your life:

> "This is a person who draws only on information from the limited resources of rational, analytic thinking without incorporating either the emotional or spiritual aspects of life. Intellectuals seldom have a holistic assessment of a situation. Their thinking tends to be dry, lifeless, and without energy. They are limited in their scope because they trust only conventional ideas. They are often judgmental and narrow in their outlook." —Ambika Wauters

Journal Questions

◉ Write about a time when you used your intuitive or wise mind to overcome a challenge.

_____

_____

_____

_____

_____

_____

_____

_____

_____

_____

_____

◉   ◉   ◉

◉ Consider the ways in which Humanistic and Transpersonal therapies and chakra six balancing will you help you improve your QOL and assist you on your evolutionary path.

_____

_____

_____

_____

_____

_____

_____

_____

_____

_____

Chakras – Energy System
Transformation Stations

Chakra Seven

Sahasrara
"Thousandfold"

Evolutionary Spirituality, Evolutionary Psychology, and Chakra Seven

The seventh chakra is called *Sahasrara* which means "thousand-fold" or "infinite" in Sanskrit. Sahasrara is located at the crown of the head and is referred to as the *thousand-petal lotus*. It is identified with the colors purple or violet or sometimes gold or silver. It has been depicted (and seen by intuitives) as a shimmering dome of white light or rainbow-colored, luminous, iridescent light. The thousand-fold or infinite lotus petals continually unfold, blossom, or cascade out into the infinite, connecting the individual self to the Higher Self. The associated element for Sahasrara is consciousness. Consciousness simply put is *thought* and includes perceptions, thoughts, beliefs, opinions, volition, and senses. Sahasrara is depicted in religious art as a halo or crown that provides respectful cover for the area of the body that connects to God. This is represented in various cultures as a hat, such as the Pope's zucchetto and the Jewish kippah or yarmulke.

Most practitioners of consciousness-raising activities experience crown chakra openings or activation as tingling sensations of the scalp. For some, the crown chakra activation can be an intense pressure that borders on pain; however, working on each chakra in ascending order with equal effort prevents discomfort. For novices and masters alike, merely visualizing infinitely cascading, luminous petals rouses the *knowing* that is Sahasrara's function.

Sahasrara governs the right *to know*. As human beings, it is our right to know we are more than flesh and blood. We have a right to know beyond any doubt that we are spiritual, universal, or celestial beings; that we are the immortal Alpha and Omega, connected to the Source of *all* that is. We have the right to experience ourselves as the infinite beings Sahasrara shows us we are. We realize higher consciousness with a balanced chakra system and Sahasrara, thus becomes the controller of all chakras, managing the entire nervous system by way of the brain's cerebral cortex.

> Sahasrara governs the right *to know*. As human beings, it is our right to know we are more than flesh and blood. We have a right to know beyond any doubt that we are spiritual, universal, or celestial beings; that we are the immortal Alpha and Omega, connected to the Source of *all* that is.

Unlike chakras one through six, the cerebral cortex has no connecting plexus, or nerve bundle. Chakra seven's location is sometimes debated, however most systems (including Hindu, Tibetan, and now Western) depict the image of Sahasrara about four-finger widths above the top of the head. This location is considered the *true crown*.

Given Sahasrara's location, views vary as to the pineal gland's proper association, chakra six or chakra seven. As discussed in Chapter 7, the pineal gland is often called the "third eye," placing it under the jurisdiction of chakra six. But chakra functions may overlap one another, and the more accepted belief is the pineal gland is integral to chakras six *and* seven.

The pineal gland secretes hormones, especially melatonin, that regulate the nervous system, govern sleep, and control our sense of peace and tranquility. In earlier species of evolution and some living reptilian species, this gland is recognized as having photoreceptor cells very similar to the light receptor cells in the human eye. There is some speculation that the pineal gland actually produces the psychedelic dimethyltryptamine (DMT), and some suggest. (there are practices to facilitate this) that the pineal gland is actually crystalizing in humans. This is not the same as the calcification process that occurs with aging; it is considered to be a biological evolutionary shift for Homo sapiens. The main function of the crystallization is to act as a radio receiver. Nonetheless, we already know Sahasrara's main function is enhanced knowing, and that brings us back to chakra seven. With chakra seven, the development of *knowing* is not sensory, intellectual, or emotional. It is *supra*-natural—beyond description. *Knowing* is an all-permeating sensation that all is well, despite life's circumstances. The comfort and safety that this feeling imparts connects to the safety established by the first chakra.

With chakra seven, the development of *knowing* is not sensory, intellectual, or emotional. It is *supra*-natural—beyond description. *Knowing* is an all-permeating sensation that all is well, despite life's circumstances. The comfort and safety that this feeling imparts connects to the safety established by the first chakra.

Sahasrara erases the differential of what is spiritual and what is not; thus, *everything* is spiritual. Its seed sound is OM with focus on the silence that follows the sound. The rule of the ego is completely broken through the embrace of the seventh chakra. Our answer to life is simply "yes." There is acceptance with no need to ask why. There is an understanding without words. We say "yes" to what we know to be our path. True discernment is attainable at this level. Our purpose in life becomes clearer, and we feel protected and guided by a power greater than ourselves. We are healthier, more resilient, freer, and filled with tremendous gratitude for what is. Our mindset is one of full and complete connection with the ultimate consciousness. We can unequivocally report, "All is One," and "It's all good." The higher consciousness that we are able to access through our seventh chakra becomes our guiding force. We develop our abilities to "let go and let God" and find the sacred in the mundane. The contemporary New Age mantra "thoughts become things" begins to make sense and manifesting our dreams becomes effortless. When we arrive at Sahasrara, we are ready for a new mode of being—*enlightenment.*

> The higher consciousness we are able to access through our seventh chakra becomes our guiding force.
> We develop our abilities to "let go and let God"
> and find the sacred in the mundane.

There is a buzz in the spiritual community that the meaning of enlightenment itself is *evolving.* Carter Phipps (1968–) a former editor of EnlightenNext magazine, and the author of the new release, *Evolutionaries,* says, "We are not just being, we are becoming."[28] For him and other forward thinkers like Hubbard, we are on the brink of a huge planetary shift that calls for immediate and conscious action. Enlightenment is being redefined as a new, practical, and meaningful necessity for survival. This ideology is taking hold across the globe, thanks in large part to the efforts of Andrew Cohen. In his new book, *Evolutionary Enlightenment,* Cohen reminds us we were there when the big bang happened. Literally. *We were there at the dawn of creation.* Once we come to know that place of *no-thingness* through chakra-work (especially as we have seen when combined with psychological consciousness-raising), meditation, and other traditional enlightenment paths, we need to know why. In other words once we can answer, "Who am I?" most of us want to know why and how we came into being. For Cohen, "Something is coming from nothing every second… in and through each and every one of us."[29]

> "The essence of the new enlightenment, which I call
> Evolutionary Enlightenment, is found in that precise moment
> when nothing became something. This is the revelation that
> liberates: that *in your very own experience* you can find that same
> vibration – the same energy, the creative tension that initiated
> the entire process at the very beginning."[30]
> **—Andrew Cohen**

No longer do we need to retreat to the caves of Tibet or a monastic life to achieve enlightenment because enlightenment seems to be coming to us. New frequencies for healing, growth, change, and knowledge are more readily available to us through evolution's own evolvement. The new Evolutionary Enlightenment is a continuous and ongoing unfolding of consciousness and creation. The impulse of evolution is the who, why, what, and how of creation.

> "As you awaken to the wild and impersonal nature of the
> evolutionary impulse, as your Authentic Self, you recognize
> more and more deeply that it is literally up to you to refine
> that God-energy through the spiritual development of your
> own soul. That is the most profound realization: that your
> own development is the evolution of God in manifest form.
> In the end, spiritual development is not your development: it
> is the evolution of God through you."[31]
> **—Andrew Cohen**

Words of wisdom, provocative concepts, and new philosophical paradigms like those that Cohen describes are being birthed, some say downloaded, into the collective at dizzying rates. Around the world, authors, artists, and healers of all modalities are creating aha moments.

People from all walks of life and cultures are joining together in record numbers to pray for peace and the healing and protection of mother Earth. The hundredth monkey phenomenon (spontaneous learning by others once a critical number, represented as "100" have learned the same thing) is undeniable as multitudes *wake up*. Futurists and evolutionaries concur this exponential expansion of consciousness signals we are on the brink of a huge leap in evolution, fueled in part by the global reach and acceptance of the Internet and the emergence of the noosphere.

The noosphere is the telepathic thinking layer of Earth. It has been likened to the Earth's central nervous system. Vladimir Vernadsky (1863–1945), a Russian-born scientist and theoretician, first introduced the concept. He proposed that the biosphere is evolving into the noosphere—its thinking layer. The noosphere concept was made popular by Pierre Teilhard de Chardin (1881–1955). Teilhard was a Jesuit priest who was denounced by Catholic officials for his teachings on evolution. The reprimand failed to quash Teilhard's work, and today his writings about the formation of the noosphere, his Law of Complexity/Consciousness, and his vision of the Omega Point echo throughout the New Age community and evolutionary circles.

> Light, energy, and information will soon redefine as commonplace, spontaneous miraculous healings and permanent improvements in our QOL. As we continue to explore the interconnectedness of the universe and discover that we are truly divine, we are all One and one with *all*, we can thank psychology, science, and religion equally.

Scientists are documenting new electromagnetic and thermodynamic frequencies of healing energy available to us through the noosphere. Light, energy, and information will soon redefine as commonplace, spontaneous miraculous healings and permanent improvements in our QOL. As we continue to explore the interconnectedness of the universe and discover that we are truly divine, we are all One and one with *all*, we can thank psychology, science, and religion equally.

Evolutionary Spirituality

Evolutionary spirituality is as much an emerging global social movement, as it is an approach to life grounded in the belief that the innate impulse to evolve is a spiritual impulse. It is best known because of Sri Aurobindo (1872–1950), one of India's most prominent leaders, first politically and then spiritually. He is regarded as an Evolutionary and is world-renowned for his teachings. His basic tenet is that man is to transcend himself (become divine), and once we develop our higher mind, we will have a "luminous thought-mind" with elevated powers and mental sight. He was describing the crown chakra being open and functioning properly.

Pir Vilayat Inayat Khan (1916-2004) was perhaps this century's greatest Sufi teacher. He taught Universal Sufism; however, he studied

"Pir Vilayat put forward an evolutionary spirituality, based on a recognition that our role as humans is to participate fully in the process by which the intelligence of the universe is awakening over time *through us*. In his view, the knowledge and insight generated from the expansion of consciousness have the potential to influence the course of evolution itself. And Pir Vilayat believed that while we are already the expression of an evolved and complex civilization, through our dynamic creativity and engagement humanity can ultimately rise to new and higher orders of existence. 'The further you advance,' he said, 'the further the horizon recedes, so the secret treasure keeps on moving further and further away. It's a very curious thing, but *we're* creating the secret. It's not there. It's like the future—we create it.'"[32]

many mystical traditions, keeping the main teaching that "all religions are rays of light from the same sun." Universality and connection to the divine are indicators that the seventh chakra is spinning in its perfect direction.

Breakthroughs in quantum physics have opened new worlds in the field of consciousness. In the article "Finding the Spirit in the Fabric of Space & Time," Tom Huston writes about the model of consciousness being developed by physicist Sir Roger Penrose (1931–) and consciousness researcher Stuart Hameroff, M.D. (1947–). They are combining Penrose's theory of quantum gravity and Hameroff's theory of quantum superposition among microtubules in the brain, and developing a theory of quantum spacetime geometry. This theory bridges the gap between science and spirituality because its hypothesis, interconnectedness amongst all things, indicates "divine guidance or cosmic wisdom influencing our choices ... and [proving] consciousness persisting outside of the body or after death."

"Consciousness is dancing on the edge, or is a process on the edge, between the quantum and classical worlds. So, spiritual practices such as meditation allow you to dive deep and become immersed in that quantum Platonic world of wisdom and light, which is the foundation of all things, both mental and material. You could even call it God if you wanted to."

Conscious Evolutionary Psychology

The field of evolutionary psychology is the scientific study of human adaptations, specifically, the neurobiological functions of the nervous system and the brain functions of language, memory, and perception with some focus on behavior. However, science is recognizing there is more to us than our biology and even more than our biology in conjunction with behavior. It is generally understood the advent of *thought* earned us the name Homo sapiens—wise man. To take us to the next phase of evolution, we need to recognize we not only *have* thought, but we *are* thought! We must consciously *think* how we want to evolve. To survive, it is imperative we create a sustainable, peaceful, productive world. The idea or the call to create the next great movement in psychology, its fifth wave, is therefore an imperative. The message that we are capable of change and we must change in order to survive must be heard by all.

To qualify as Conscious Evolutionary Psychology, (refer to glossary of terms) a theoretical framework must meet five criteria. It must incorporate an evolutionary trajectory, employ consciousness-raising activities, utilize an eclectic combination of standard psychiatric and

> To take us to the next phase of evolution, we need to recognize we not only *have* thought, but we *are* thought! We must consciously *think* how we want to evolve. To survive, it is imperative we create a sustainable, peaceful, productive world. The idea or the call to create the next great movement in psychology, its fifth wave, is therefore an imperative. The message that we are capable of change and we must change in order to survive must be heard by all.

psychological frameworks, demonstrate a comprehensive understanding of spirituality, and use state-of-the-art energy healing modalities. The latest developments in the fields of quantum physics, energy medicine, and new psychological theoretical frameworks like Unitive, Integral, and Celestial Psychology show promise that a new wave of Conscious Evolutionary Psychology will make its mark and become the fifth wave of psychology and psychological theory.

A discussion of Conscious Evolutionary Psychology begins by taking a look at the work of one of the world's most influential evolutionaries, Barbara Marx Hubbard (1929–). At this writing, Hubbard is in her early 80s, and remains a role model for a rich and meaningful life. As a teen, she was disturbed by the dropping of the nuclear bomb on Hiroshima, and she began asking the question, "Now that we know how destructive we can be as a species, what's good about us?" Not even then-President Eisenhower was able to give her an answer when she posed the question to him during a White House interview in 1952. This question began her life's work and she remains a major contributor to the fields of evolution, Evolutionary Spirituality, and the newly evolving Conscious Evolutionary Psychology. Hubbard studied with Sri Aurobindo and was influenced by great thinkers like Teilhard de Chardin, Buckminster Fuller (1895-1983), and Abraham Maslow. Maslow befriended her and they spent hours discussing the meaning of life, actualization of the self, and evolution of mankind. She has written a number of books and is most famous for *Conscious Evolution: Awakening the Power of Our Social Potential*. She is best known as a futurist and she insists that:

> "We are one body, born into the Universe, discovering greater awareness of our Creative Intention... We are at the dawn of 'conscious evolution,' when the creature-human first becomes aware of the processes of creation and begins to participate deliberately in the design of our world."[33]
> —**Barbara Marx Hubbard**

Hubbard's work meets four of the five criteria for the fifth wave psychology, although it is not a psychological theory. She offers self-help courses that incorporate consciousness-raising, and online courses, such as Ego to Essence training, that prepare the individual for spiritual evolvement and provide leadership training for Evolutionaries. An example of the latter is "Agents of Conscious Evolution" (ACE) training. Her courses feature energetic breathwork and chakra meditations.

Unitive Psychology

Unitive Psychology, created by Dr. Albert LaChance, (19xx–) can be placed into the Conscious Evolutionary Psychology category because it is concerned with the growth and development of the individual *Homo sapiens* into the *Homo spiritus*. LaChance states that universal "consciousness has four sequential phases in the human known as *Homo instinctus* (the tribal), *Homo affectus* (the religious), *Homo rationalis* (the scientific/technological), and *Homo spiritus* (the Unitive)."[34] He categorizes the genetic code into four levels: propagation, ecological governance, culture, and *unitive*. The unitive level is the "...*transcendent and inclusive* level, which is the goal of the immediate future." The tremendous influx of current trends and activities, often referred to as New Age, point to the much talked about acceleration of this process. His 12th principle reads:

> "Our supreme challenge presently is to reach the fourth level of genetic coding: a Unitive BioLogos. This will be accomplished when sufficient numbers of individuals realize the Fourth Voice in themselves. This collective awakening will be the dawning in Homo-spiritus of the Unitive Period of the human/earth relationship."
> **—Dr. Albert LaChance**

The evolutionary trajectory in LaChance's theoretical framework is also illustrated by his incorporation of 12-Step facilitation, widely regarded as one of the most effective consciousness-raising frameworks ever practiced. Unitive Psychology utilizes an eclectic framework for psychotherapy, demonstrates understanding of metaphysics and contains some exercises for consciousness-raising; thus, it meets four of the five Conscious Evolutionary Psychology criteria. Although energy medicine modalities are absent from the consciousness-raising exercises, Unitive Psychology qualifies on the strength of its compliance with the other criteria.

Integral Psychology

Integral Psychology is the name that Ken Wilber calls his theory of psychology. This theory concerns itself with the spiritual health of the individual and the evolution of the species. Wilber's work includes analyses of numerous schools of psychology and spirituality, and using his Integral Approach to philosophy, collates them in an integrated synthesis. The work is hailed as the integrating force merging Eastern and Western psycho-spiritual worldviews. Wilber developed the Ten Fulcrums of Consciousness to outline the psyche of man. He has also made the concept of enlightenment, which is typically thought of as a spiritual pursuit, into a goal for everyone's human development. Wilber founded Integral Life, a community for leaders, artists, and anyone with a vision for a better future. This community offers numerous paths of study and different consciousness-raising techniques. Thus, Integral Psychology meets four out of five criteria to be considered a Conscious Evolutionary Psychology, lacking only the incorporation of energy medicine modalities. Just as with Unitive Psychology, Integral Psychology qualifies on the strength of those four criteria.

Integral Life Mission Statement

"An integral life is total freedom to be who you already are.
A life where peace and passion come alive.
Providing a place for everything in your life.
Better relationships, sex, career and health.
More effectiveness, more purpose.
Less confusion, less fear.
In order to be. And to become.
Welcome to Integral Life.
Where growth enthusiasts make sense of everything."

Celestial Psychology

Celestial Psychology ("CP") fits into the newly emerging category of Conscious Evolutionary Psychology by meeting all required criteria. CP incorporates an evolutionary trajectory not only in principal, but also in practical application with affirmations, assigned reading, and writing exercises. Further, CP is experiential with consciousness-raising activities that are drawn from various world religions, metaphysics, energy medicine modalities, and spiritual practices including chakra-balancing. By utilizing an eclectic combination of standard psychiatric and psychological applications, and keeping up with the latest state-of-the-art healing modalities, such as the Reconnection, CP qualifies as a Conscious Evolutionary Psychology.

Celestial Psychology holds promise as the leading theoretical framework for the psychology of a new era of humanity being referred to as the New Humanity. Learning to harmonize higher vibrational frequencies and activate the subtle bodies through chakra-balancing with a psychotherapeutic theoretical orientation will become commonplace in the near future.

"Healing our mind is the same as healing our energy. We learn to love and accept what makes us unique, and to forgive ourselves for the times we diminished our worth and honor our choices for love."
—**Ambika Wauters**

Celestial Psychology® holds promise as the leading theoretical framework for the psychology of the New Humanity. Learning to harmonize higher vibrational frequencies and activate the subtle bodies through chakra-balancing with a psychotherapeutic theoretical orientation will become commonplace in the near future.

Physiological Signs of Chakra Seven Imbalance

The areas of the body governed by the Seventh Chakra are brain stem, nervous system, spinal cord, pineal gland, cerebral cortex. This chakra regulates the entire hormonal system, but especially controls the production of melatonin. Comas, migraines, brain tumors, or amnesia, are indicators of chakra seven imbalance

Psychological Signs of Chakra Seven Imbalance

Common symptoms include cognitive delusions and dark nights of the soul. Severe and/or radical spiritual abandonment or the opposite severe and radical attachments are symptoms of chakra seven imbalance. Loss of identity and connection to self and others that manifests in confusion and loneliness is common also. Uncommon and more severe symptoms include Schizophrenia, extraordinary isolation, and dissociative states associated with borderline and multiple-personality disorders.

Therapeutic Focus

Combine chakra-balancing techniques with an examination of belief systems, eliminating the limiting and negative ones. Focus on working towards letting go of everything. Practice radical acceptance and random acts of kindness. Avoid asking questions like "Who am I?" and "Why am I here?" and practice *knowing* the answer.. Shift from religious orientation to spiritual orientation. Practice mindfulness, meditation, yoga, and any other spiritual practices that require discipline. Develop an intuitive sense of connection. Develop the objective observer, the inner witness.

⬤Notes

_____

_____

_____

_____

_____

_____

_____

_____

_____

Chakra Seven Properties

Location ....Top of the skull

Age of resonance.....................42-49

Shape..Round skullcap

Glandular Connection.............Pineal gland, which
secretes melatonin and
other hormones know to
affect tranquility, sleep,
and light sensitivity

Color...Violet

Musical note............................B

Type of Music ....Indian ragas

Element....................................The Cosmos

Aspect of intelligence ....Spiritual understanding

Sensory experience ....Bliss

Essential oils ....Violet, lavender, lotus,
elemi

Crystals....................................Amethyst, alexandrite

Aspects of the Solar System....The Universe

Astrological associations ....Aquarius

Chakra Seven Properties

Metal .... Platinum

Earthly Locations .... India

Mythological animal .... Eagle

Plant .... Lotus flower

Qualities .... Grace, beauty, serenity, oneness with all that is

Life issues .... Selfless realization of your indelible connection with the greater whole of life; creation of a vital and resilient spiritual context for holding your life experiences

Physical activities .... None- stillness

Spiritual activities .... Prayer, meditation, reflection

Positive archetype .... Guru

Negative archetype .... Egotist

Angelic presence .... The Christ Light

—Ambika Wauters
The Book of Chakras: Discover the Hidden Forces Within You

Healing Stones

Diamond, Spirit Quartz, Tanzanite, Purple Sapphire, Achroite (Colorless Tourmaline), Amethyst, Clear Calcite, Clear Quartz, Herkimer, Halite, Clear Topaz, White Sapphire White Jade, Selenite, Angel's Wing (Fishtail Selenite), Selenite Phantom

Amethyst Crystal Natural Formation

Suggested Yoga Postures for Chakra Seven

English	Sanskrit
Seating Posture	*Yoga Mudra*
Fish	*Matsayana*

● Notes

_____

_____

_____

_____

_____

_____

_____

_____

Meditation for Opening the Crown Chakra

 Warning: It is important to develop a strong root chakra BEFORE using this meditation.

● Review Sahasrara's functions.

● Sit comfortably with your spine straight and focus your attention on the area of your crown at the top of your head, up and to three inches above your skull.

MUDRA FOR OPENING CROWN CHAKRA

● Clasp your hands with fingers crossed inside and left thumb underneath the right. Raise your ring fingers to form a crown. Raise your hands over your head, in front of your solar plexus, or rest them on your lap.

● Inhale deeply and as you exhale chant the mantra NG three times. (Suggested musical note–B)

● Repeat for 7 to 10 breaths.

 Free form chant along with Baird Hersey's Chakra Seven "White Light" Waking the Cobra: Vocal Meditations on the Chakras

● Notes

_____

_____

_____

_____

_____

_____

Short Affirmation

**I am transcended
because the seventh chakra
of my energetic/spiritual body
is activated, open and alive.**

*Memorize and repeat 3x in a row
at least 3x per day.*

Evolutionary Affirmation

I am transcended. I am free from the trappings of the egoic mind. I am timeless and eternal. I am the source of everything. I have no beginning and I have no ending. I am all that ever was and I am all that ever will be. I am the infinite potentiality, the inexhaustible possibility. My flow is eternal, all-reaching, unhindered by time or space. I am one with the infinite. My

seventh chakra is balanced and spinning in its perfect direction for where I am right now, working toward my evolution, strengthening my celestial body, creating my Homo-luminous being.

*Read 1x per day while relaxed,
preferably after completing the meditations.*

Guided Visualization

Sit in a comfortable straight-backed chair. Imagine you are sitting on the most magnificent throne you can imagine. You are surrounded by angels with wings of the brightest and most celestial white you have ever seen. A jeweled crown is placed on your head, which casts a golden radiance all around your head. You are adorned in brilliant opalescent

garments with intricate designs woven of glittering silver thread.

You feel the strongest spiritual connection you have ever felt. You feel the presence of the highest spiritual beings you've ever known. The love that emanates from them comforts you beyond any comfort you've ever known. Their love for you is compelling you to remember that it's always

been there and will always be there. You are both the lover and the beloved. You are cherished and adored ... you are absolutely, divinely perfect. You trust that your seventh chakra is compelling you to transcend into your Homo-luminous self.

You trust that you are evolving.

You enjoy the process.

You enjoy your life.

Celestial Psychology Principles: Chakra Seven

Holy Work is the responsibility of the individual; however, when being performed or practiced, it's efficacy is enhanced by the individual's focus on divine or celestial forces, which are omniscient and omnipresent.

Human/spiritual/celestial beings are at their best when serving others

Meditate on these principles.
Then journal with free association.

Notes

Journal Questions

After completing any of the exercises above, remain
relaxed to answer the following questions.
Use free association.
Write your immediate response.
After answering "yes" or "no,"
add a brief explanation.
Don't overthink your answers.

Am I aware of the spiritual?

_____
_____
_____
_____
_____

Am I disciplined in whatever practice I engage in?

_____
_____
_____
_____
_____

Am I guided by my Higher Power?

_____
_____
_____
_____
_____

Journal Questions

● Do I honor and value beauty?

_____

_____

_____

_____

_____

● Do I transcend my belief system?

_____

_____

_____

_____

_____

● Do I know my essential self?

_____

_____

_____

_____

_____

● Do I consider the good of all?

_____

_____

_____

_____

_____

Journal Questions

Consider the ways in which the positive archetype of The Guru may be influencing you:

> "Gurus are people who realize who they are. They know that the divine force flows through them and they are identified with that as the substratum of their being, rather than the temporal parts of their life. They let life move through them and take them ever deeper into consciousness itself." –Ambika Wauters

Consider the ways in which the negative archetype of The Egotist may be influencing your life:

> "Egotists are people who think their efforts alone carry them through life. They believe that they are separate from a greater whole of existence and that their striving and effort controls the outcome of their life." –Ambika Wauters

Journal Questions

⬤ Let your imagination soar and write about life in the future, including what you see as the New Humanity? Be sure to include your contributions to date.

_____

_____

_____

_____

_____

_____

_____

_____

_____

_____

⬤ Consider the ways in which Conscious Evolutionary therapies and chakra seven balancing will help you improve your QOL.

_____

_____

_____

_____

_____

_____

_____

_____

_____

_____

_____

_____

CHAPTER 10

Celestial ● Psychology®
and the Fifth Wave

Nothing in this lifetime of study and first-hand experience has elevated me to new dimensions the way preparing this workbook has. And yet, above all else it has increased my optimism for you—reader, student, teacher, or healer—that you now have more tools to help you elevate your consciousness and wake up to new dimensions of yourself. I am confident that the concepts and exercises presented in these pages have provided something for everyone to assist in spiritual empowerment and the ability to say, "Yes!" to life in a new way.

By saying "Yes!" to completing this workbook and the ensuing companion text (release date Summer 2013) I continue to push myself beyond my comfort zone. I now understand the *Work* is working me, because it is a timely and exceedingly important opportunity to not only ensure optimal mental health for myself, but also for you and for generations to come. I am optimistic that the *Work* is now working you, helping you find answers and your place in this perhaps, not so crazy, after all, 'crazy world of ours.'

I am confident also that you now see, the *Holy Work* of consciousness-raising with Celestial Psychology wakes us up. It ignites a flame that begins to push us beyond our comfort zones with the profound sense of urgency we've come to know as the driver of evolution, the evolutionary trajectory.

This evolutionary trajectory is the impulse of evolution itself. It is the infinite, incessant, forward-moving pulse of creation. Its speed and intensity accelerate every time we acknowledge it. Its frequency increases when we facilitate it. It flows into every aspect of being, from our DNA to infinite space, whenever we ask it to. It reveals luminosity, figuratively and sometimes literally, every time we request to see the light. By its very nature it assists in all healing efforts by opening us to Itself and providing all the information we need to create miracles, to accomplish the impossible, and to say, "Yes!" to life.

> The *Holy Work* of consciousness-raising with Celestial Psychology wakes us up. It ignites a flame that begins to push us beyond our comfort zones with the profound sense of urgency we've come to know as the driver of evolution, the evolutionary trajectory.

I also believe the call for a new movement in psychology—its fifth wave—is a call for all disciplines to incorporate energy medicine and an evolutionary trajectory into their work. Psychologists, psychiatrists, social workers, nurses, and healers of all disciplines must pull together and instill hope as we face the reality that we possess the means to destroy ourselves. We must be able to state unequivocally we are entering into a time of great shift that is positive. We must proclaim along with the greatest philosophers and thinkers of our time, and the world's greatest prophets and indigenous elders throughout all time-this is a new era of humanity and it is the most important time in history for the species of Homo sapiens. Thus, declaring Conscious Evolutionary Psychology as the fifth wave of psychology provides another vehicle of change necessary to carry us into this next phase of human development.

Whether you are a professional in the healing arts or a layperson, I have faith that you now share my conviction that we must elevate our minds and bodies to spirit in order to survive—individually and collectively. We must allow and encourage the imaginal cells among us to thrive. We all must carry the message and manifest the reality that human beings are capable of change beyond our wildest dreams by raising consciousness. This way we will hold on to the glorious vision of the new human, whether we choose to call ourselves Homo luminous, Homo universalis, or Homo angelicus. Most important, we must strive to cooperate more fully, love more completely, and care more deeply for each other, ourselves, and Gaia, our Mother Earth.

"This structure, the extra-cellular matrix, [microtubules, actin and protein filaments] has been called a "missing organ" in our understanding of physiology, and has been well studied and described by James Oschman. Given that we now understand the meridians [and chakras] to be "pathways of light," we can truly say we are "light beings."

> ## This is not just New Age mumbo-jumbo; it is solid science."[35]
> —James Oschman

Glossary

Akashic Record has been referred to as God's book of knowledge or remembrance, however, today it is more commonly understood to be energetic imprints on the astral plane, ether or akasha which is Sanskrit for sky. Theosophical scholars believe that every thought, word and deed is recorded and can be accessed while in altered states of consciousness.

Altered states or non-ordinary states of consciousness were first acknowledged by Abraham Maslow as legitimate opportunities for healing the mind, body and spirit, whether spontaneous or deliberately induced, rather than pathological or psychotic states as previously considered. Stanislov Grof calls non-ordinary states Holotropic. He has devoted his whole career to researching psychedelic drugs, shamanism, Buddhism, Taoism, and meditation-induced dimensions of the psyche.

Ananda is Indian for the bliss of being.

Ascended Masters are human beings that are no longer living in the physical world, but are living (some still in their physical bodies) in heaven or the fifth, sixth, or higher dimensions.

Ascension is literally the act of moving up. In traditional religious teaching, it's the physical body of the master (Jesus or Muhammad, et al) that actually ascended into heaven, thus, transcending death. In less traditional religious teachings, the "good" people will ascend, as in Rapture. In New Age terms, it is not always taken literally and can refer to the development of a human light body capable of transcending suffering and a peaceful thriving planet.

Atman is a Sanskrit term for God within or the spiritual life of the individual as well as the universe, i.e., the essence of the soul or all that is eternal. It is the opposite of Maya the illusion of reality.

Aura is the energy field or luminous radiation around matter that is not visible to most people (psychics sometimes have this ability) with the naked eye. Kirlian photography can capture the varying degrees of color in the aura around living objects.

Auric field is sometimes referred to as the layers of consciousness that surround the physical body.

Axiotonal Lines are a grid system of lines around and through the physical body, the earth, and beyond into the universe.

Celestial Psychology® is an eclectic blend of: standard, well-known psychotherapeutic theories; psychiatric, nutritional, and energy medicine interventions; a variety of consciousness-raising techniques, including but not limited to utilization of affirmations, visualizations, guided meditations and journal writing. Celestial Psychology is founded on the basic principle that human beings are capable of change. Especially by consciously and deliberately evolving into higher beings, and that this evolvement process is essential to the survival of the species.

Chakra(s) are the energetic force fields, where spiritual, psychological and physical qualities in the body merge, blend and transform. Chakra in Sanskrit means wheel. The spokes of the wheel that emanate from each chakra's center spin with varying intensity, and can be activated by focusing on them, especially with meditation and yoga. The major chakras are located in the body along the spine and they can't be seen, they can only be experienced. However, intuitives and special computerized readings confirm that chakras are real and are identifiable by their universally accepted corresponding colors.

Cognitive Therapy originated with the work of Albert Ellis and Aaron Beck. It is widely used today and includes Cognitive Behavioral Therapies, and Cognitive Restructuring Therapy. It is founded on the premise that irrational thoughts and negative beliefs contribute to depressive states, thereby contributing to unacceptable behavior.

Conscious Evolution is the idea that Homo sapiens are becoming conscious of the creative power of consciousness, itself. Now, at a critical time in history human beings must, for the first time make choices that consciously and deliberately evolve themselves and the planet. Capable of choice through the liberation of consciousness Homo sapiens are waking up and realizing- we are capable of co-creating a sustainable future for the species and the planet, and we are capable of creating heaven on Earth.

Conscious Evolutionary Psychology is the newly emerging fifth wave of psychology. In order to qualify as a Conscious Evolutionary Psychology the theoretical framework must incorporate the following five criteria:

❖ incorporate an evolutionary trajectory;

❖ utilize an eclectic combination of standard psychiatric and psychological frameworks with psychotherapy (talk therapy);

❖ demonstrate a comprehensive understanding of the world's religions, metaphysics, the occult, and all things pertaining to the New Age;

❖ employ consciousness-raising activities, such as meditation and the use of affirmations and visualizations;

❖ apply the latest state-of-the-art energy healing modalities – including but not limited to: chakra-balancing, Reiki, Therapeutic Touch and other hands-on healing modalities, Reconnection® Healing Practices, Pranic Healing, Emotional Freedom Technique (EFT), Shamanism or any combination thereof.

Consciousness simply put, (albeit far from simple) is what we "know" and how we know it. It is derived from the Latin verb scire - to know and the Latin preposition con, meaning with. It is the awareness that one exists, as well as the quality of being aware of existence and/or aware of one's surroundings. This includes subjective experiences such as, mental states, perceptions, thoughts, beliefs, opinions, volition and all the senses. It is both one's internal cosmos and the cosmos itself. Quantum physics is developing a growing body of evidence supporting the religious/spiritual paradigm that consciousness is in fact, literally what God is, therefore, God resides within human beings, as well as, outside of human beings.

Consciousness-raising is the practice of making conscious what's unconscious. It is the desired outcome of all bio-psycho-social-spiritual therapeutic interventions regardless of theoretical orientation. In biological circles the act of focusing on healing is an act of consciousness-raising. In psychological circles consciousness-raising encompasses all interventions. In social circles consciousness-raising for the collective, is usually associated with a liberation movement, such as, the Women's Liberation Movement. In spiritual circles, raising consciousness is accomplished by focusing on any or all of the following; angels, saints, ascended masters, God or a Higher Power, or the ethereal, energetic body as in the chakra system.

Dimensions (of consciousness) are levels of reality which correspond to different planes of existence. Philosophers, scholars and metaphysicians generally agree there are five planes or dimensions, however, there is growing consensus that twelve or fifteen levels actually exist in the universe. Dimensions progress from physical to divine and vibrate at different frequencies and are governed by specific principles and universal laws. Homo sapiens exist in the third dimension and are evolving into higher or multi-dimensional beings.

Divination is any form of foretelling the future or determining the present or the past through insight obtained with supernatural powers usually through oracles, obtaining omens, reading tea leaves, Tarot cards, or the I Ching (book of ancient Chinese wisdom). Different cultures utilize their own forms, although technology and the onset of the New Age has developed cross-culture usage and there has been an incredible influx of new and creative tools being marketed to the general public.

Diviners is a more contemporary term for oracles. Some diviners use magnetic devices similar to dowsing rods to measure the positive or negative energy in a room, or person's aura.

Divine/Energy Matrix or Field of Consciousness is the unified field of existence in which all intelligence/information is stored and from which we derive transformative powers.

Divine Mind from a spiritual, non-denominational perspective is generally understood to be the upper case "S" in Self.

Ego - Edges God or Goodness Out. Ego, according to contemporary thinkers is the lower case "s" in self; it is the "false" self; it is considered the source of mankind's suffering. It is the dream or maya, the illusion of who and what we really are.

Egoic mind is all of consciousness - individual and collective that is not Atman, or Divine Mind, i.e., it is all that Edges God or Goodness Out. It is the part of mankind that identifies solely with itself, as if there is absolutely nothing else.

Egoist, the (negative archetype) Egoists believe in the separation of self and existence or divinity. They believe only their own efforts control their lives.

Emotive telepathy is a term from parapsychology that indicates kinesthetic sensations are transferrable.

Energy Medicine is the term that became known in the early eighties for the branch of alternative or complementary medicine, which utilizes subtle, putative energies, or light to heal. Healing with subtle energies is documented throughout history and in all indigenous cultures. The Chinese system of acupuncture is based on directing the flow of the subtle or vital energy they named, Chi or Qi (pronounced Chee). Jesus Christ remains the world's most renowned healer, although, not typically considered an energy medicine practitioner, it is generally understood that he utilized light to heal.. Energy medicine is becoming mainstream and includes a wide variety of modalities, such as acupuncture, acupressure, chakra-balancing, Reiki (offered in many mainstream hospitals), the Reconnection®, Pranic healing, Emotional Freedom Technique (EFT), Shamanism or any combination thereof.

Enlightenment has heretofore been considered a state of being reserved for mystics, monks, or yogis, achieved through rigorous meditation practices. This state of being, called Satori in Sanskrit, consists of total immersion into higher states of consciousness. This higher or altered state is considered to be a permanent achievement for these very rare individuals. Today, thanks to philosophers like Ken Wilber and Andrew Cohen, Enlightenment is not only considered an achievable goal for everyone, it has become known as part of mankind's innate Evolutionary Impulse.

Esoteric is the term that points to the 'internal' world. It is associated with spirituality, metaphysics and the occult, i.e., all things that are considered hidden or secret.

Ethereal is most often used to refer to things that are airy, other worldly or out of this atmosphere, and is sometimes used to describe a layer or dimension of consciousness.

Exoteric is a term that points to the 'external' world. It would thus be associated with religious teachings that have to do with dogma and external rules.

Evolution has come to mean more than the biological paradigm of Darwinism. In today's evolving paradigm, the evolutionary process includes the development of consciousness- which is becoming understood to be the ultimate component to our survival as a species.

Evolutionary is an individual who accepts that evolution is a spiritual process; understands that the transformation of our world depends on our willingness to deliberately and consciously evolve ourselves; understands that the survival of our species and our planet is dependent on evolution; and is committed to the evolutionary process.

Evolutionary eyes develop once we accept the newly evolving esoteric paradigm mentioned above. Everything we observe becomes a function of the process. All disasters both man-made and natural, all struggles, aches and pains begin to make sense as we understand that negativity comes to the surface for its purification and purification is the natural order.

Evolutionary Psychology has traditionally been a branch of science that consists of the study of human adaptations. Specifically, neurobiological functions of the nervous system, the brain functions of language, memory, perception and behavior.

Evolutionary Spirituality is both a global social movement in its beginning stages, as well as a concept that purports that the innate impulse to evolve is a spiritual impulse.

Evolutionary trajectory becomes the way we begin to understand all the movement in the universe. It is a forward moving thrust providing sense and direction for a positive future (no matter the appearance of the present).

Evolutionary worldview did not exist before the 1930s. Over the last eighty years or so, there has been an exponentially growing awareness that consciousness and evolution are nearly synonymous. As each individual develops his or her evolutionary eyes, the evolutionary worldview develops in the collective unconscious or the noosphere.

Existentialism is the philosophical movement that led to the Existential Therapies made popular by Irvin Yalom. Yalom realized that man's quest to understand existence, and to find meaning in life are foundational to all theoretical frameworks for psychotherapy. The existentialist concepts of freedom, responsibility, individuality and authenticity are inherent in all pursuits to improve the QOL factor.

Finder is any individual who has stopped seeking and knows beyond doubt that they are an evolving spiritual being "... no longer trying to become enlightened but have let go of any other option than to be the expression of the highest we have seen and experienced, in all our imperfection, right now. That's what it means to be a finder." Andrew Cohen (blog May 23, 2011)

First wave/force, or the first major movement of psychology to appear is considered to be psychoanalytical theories with their emphasis on the unconscious conflicts that develop beginning in childhood. This includes Jungian psychology, along with the obvious Freudian psychology. In Celestial Psychology, the Existentialist theories are included in the first wave.

Fourth wave/force, or the fourth major movement of psychology to appear is generally considered only the Transpersonal Psychologies, with Humanistic being the third wave. However, in Celestial Psychology, the Humanistic and Transpersonal are under the same umbrella- that of the fourth wave.

Fifth wave/force or the fifth major movement of psychology is now declared to be the Conscious Evolutionary Psychologies. To date, there are a few frameworks that come close, however, only Celestial Psychology meets all the criteria.

Futurist(s) are scholars, scientists, innovators or any individuals who are concerned with the future. They study historical and current trends to indicate what's coming- however, not necessarily to predict specifics.

Gestalt is a German word for the form or essence created by the things that made it up or shaped it. It is the process in psychology where the parts are brought to completeness. Thus, it is any act of completion from the simplest- as in taking a sip of water to quench a thirst- to the most complex, as in walking down the aisle to be married.

Gestalt therapy was developed by Fritz Perls who was nearly worshipped by the clinicians who studied with him at the Esalen Institute in California in the 1960s. The basic premise of Gestalt therapy is that humans are continually engaged in the process of completing themselves, or making themselves whole.

Grace is a gift of spiritual energy, regeneration or sanctification to humankind from the divine.

Guru, the (positive archetype) Any teacher or expert, usually on religious or spiritual matters who has become recognized (in some case revered) as a leader. He or she (to date this is mostly a masculine title) lives in a manner which indicates they know their own divinity, live in the flow, or the moment and mentor in a way that creates transcendence in others.

Holotropic experience is a term developed by Stanislov Grof, MD and is used to describe an altered state of consciousness where the boundaries of the ego are transcended and 'wholeness' is achieved. Grof was a proponent of using psychedelic substances, although he did create the safer, more practical breathing technique called Holotropic Breathwork, in order to achieve and maintain these perceptual changes as more permanent.

Holotropic breathwork is a breathing technique developed by Stanislav Grof, MD, utilizing rigorous controlled breathing to achieve altered or non-ordinary states of consciousness.

Holy Work is the term for the consciousness-raising activities in Celestial Psychology. Holy Work includes the use of talk-therapy, any form of meditation, ritual, ceremony, physical activity, energy medicine and energetic body-work designed to permanently improve QOL and higher states of awareness.

Homo-luminous is a term that has roots in ancient indigenous cultures and was brought to holistic circles and made popular by Alberto Viloldo, PhD. Evolutionaries believe that Homo sapiens are developing into Homo luminous light beings.

Homo universalis is a term for the species Homo sapiens that has evolved into knowing itself as One body, one with each other and one with the universe. Also indicates the species is evolving into an intergalactic cooperative existence.

Human Energy System (HES) is the anatomy of all the structures that sustain the life force or chi. This system consists of the layers or dimensions that surround the body, including the aura; the chakras - generally 7 major and hundreds of minor ones at the physical bodies joints meridian points; and energetic cords and bundles of cords, each with their highly specialized functions. Science is beginning to verify its existence, and more people are waking up to the HES via yoga, meditation or deliberate practices.

Humanistic Psychology is a theoretical framework that is based on the principles that human beings are fundamentally good and are driven to self-actualization. It is typically associated as beginning with Abraham Maslow because he was the founder of The Association of Humanistic Psychology (1961). However, it was Socrates who first recognized the necessity for self-reflection, which inevitably leads to self-actualization and much of the Humanistic Approach has its roots in Existentialism.

Idealism in relation to metaphysical principles purports that reality is incorporeal, immaterial or spiritual and/or mental in nature.

Imaginal cells are the cells of change in a biologically evolving organism. The best example are the cells that develop in the cocoon of the butterfly. These cells hold the image of what the butterfly is to become and at first they are attacked and killed off by the old cells. Eventually they outnumber the old cells and the butterfly develops unencumbered. Evolutionaries are considered the imaginal cells of the New Humanity.

Integrative Medicine (IM) takes the Western medical model and blends it with alternative or complementary treatments.

Interpersonal Psychotherapies (IPT) exists today as a twelve to sixteen visit brief therapeutic intervention. The Transactional Analysis work of Berne and Harris made Interpersonal Psychotherapies famous.

Intuition is the ability to know something instinctively, without evidence or prior learning.

Intuitives are individuals who are capable of knowing, gathering information and/or healing others (and sometimes themselves).

Intuitive telepathy is a term from parapsychology that denotes the transfer of time-based information from one individual to another. Can also be called precognitive or retrocognitive telepathy.

Journey. See SHAMANIC JOURNEY

Kundalini is the subtle or primal energy of consciousness that is reportedly lying dormant in a coiled position at the base of the spine, in the first chakra. It is depicted as a golden serpent with its tail in its own mouth. Different yoga and meditation exercises are practiced to raise the Kundalini energy up- through the chakra system, in order to experience altered states of consciousness, and even enlightenment. It is always prudent to practice with a teacher, as there have been many cases of extreme discomfort and even psychotic episodes reported as a result of raising Kundalini without proper preparation.

Latent telepathy is a term from parapsychology that denotes the lapse of time between sending and receiving transferred information.

Local Self is the term Barbara Marx Hubbard uses to describe the ego.

Magnetic Center is a concept in esoteric work that identifies a function of the higher self that governs the development of itself. Spiritual seekers and mystics could be said to have magnetic center by virtue of their predilection to be on a path, regardless of choice or progress.

Mandala loosely translated from Sanskirt means circle, however, it is used to describe complex circular works of art that are usually considered sacred. Mandalas are often used as meditation tools to stimulate heightened consciousness.

Materialism is a philosophical theory purporting that the only reality is that of physical matter. This includes considering psychological states such as emotions, reason, thought, will and desire as physical functions. Materialism precludes the existence of God.

Maya is Hindu for illusion. It is the opposite of Atman, the reality of God.

Medical intuitive is an individual who is able to intuit (either in person or long distance) correct diagnosis of medical, mental, or spiritual disease.

Medium is an individual who communicates with the spirits of the deceased, angelic beings or other otherworldly beings, by direct command, in order to obtain or convey knowledge that is unavailable by worldly methods. Ancient oracles and contemporary mediums may or may not use a divination tool, such as divining rods, cards, coins, stones, bones or others such materials.

Meridian points are electro-magnetic palpable spots located along the bodies' meridian lines. They are treated with needles (acupuncture) or pressure (acupressure) to release blocked energy and heal the body of disease. New research indicates they are not only pathways energy, but also of light and information.

Metanoia in psychology refers to a psychotic break that results in a positive psychological re-building or healing. Commonplace meaning is a change of heart, correction or repentance.

Metaphysics is the philosophical concern or branch of science that studies the fundamental nature of all reality, the seen and unseen, the visible and the invisible. It is the study of- and the subsequent describing of- being and knowing. It is concerned with whatever is the fundamental nature that anything must have in order to be.

Metaphysician or (Metaphysicist) is a student of metaphysics. However, there are a number of esoteric schools that provide in-depth studies and certifications that would lend one to declare oneself and metaphysician, as opposed to a student of metaphysics.

Metempsychosis or transmigration (contemporary term) occurs when the soul passes into another body, animal or plant, as in reincarnation.

Mindfulness Meditation is taught to train the mind to observe itself. This popular form of meditation was made main stream by John Kabat Zihn in his book, "Wherever You Go, There You Are." It has been brought into contemporary psychology, esp. by the work of Marsha Linehan, LCSW who uses it in her Dialectic Behavioral Training (DBT).

Mudra is a Sanskrit term for hand gestures or full body gestures that represent or symbolize or create connections between the spiritual and the physical body.

Mysticism is the practice of or experience of altered states of reality or consciousness that are typically associated with divine union and/or spiritual revelation, for the purpose of transformation. There are numerous religions and a variety of classified types of mysticism.

Mystical Experience is a spiritual revelation, vision or state of consciousness, typically achieved as a result of practicing mysticism in a variety of ways, including but not limited to meditation, prayer, ecstatic or trance dance, and intuition. Difficult to put into words, these experiences don't usually last more than a half-day.

Namaste is an Indian term. It is the standard greeting or farewell used by Hindus. It is typically performed by the greeter as a bow with hands at chest height in a prayerful position toward the individual being greeted.

Near Death Experience (NDE) are more prevalently reported since the invention of cardiac paddles. They are only legitimized if the individual accounting the experience was officially pronounced clinically dead.

New Age is a social movement begun in the last few decades predominantly involving taking age-old wisdom from religious, philosophical, metaphysical, and occult teachings and bringing them into today by mixing them with contemporary scientific, medical, and especially the psychological practices and insights of transpersonal psychology.

New Human. See THE NEW HUMAN

New Humanity. See THE NEW HUMANITY

Noosphere is considered by most to be the third layer of or 'sphere' of earth and it consists of human thought. (The first layer being inanimate matter known as the geosphere and the second is biological life- the biosphere.) The word noosphere was originally introduced by Vladimir Vernadsky, but it was Teilhard deChardin's Law of Complexity/Consciousness concept that is to this day bringing the term into mainstream culture. Barbara Marx Hubbard and Jose Arguelles have written extensively about it. Hubbard considers the internet to be the physical manifestation or counterpart to the ethereal web of human consciousness, which has the potential to organize itself according to our creative collective efforts, either for constructive or destructive purposes.

Past Life Regression is the practice of utilizing hypnosis to access memories of one's past lives.

Phenomenology is a branch of philosophy that studies the mind via introspection.

Pneuma is Greek for "life-force."

Prana is Sanskrit for "life-force."

Psychic is a term for an individual who engages in paranormal activity(ies), such as, telepathy and/or clairvoyance.

Psychoanalytic Psychology and Freudian Psychology are often used interchangeably, although there are a number of other psychoanalytic or neo-Freudian approaches that were developed later. Ego Psychology, Object-Relations and brief psychoanalytic psychotherapy developed over time, are more widely accepted and still often utilized today, especially, in eclectic combination with other theoretical approaches.

Psychogenic illnesses are emotionally based and real. They are not "in the patients head", as some might conjecture.

Psycho kinesis literally means mind movement and it generally refers to a variety of mental or psychic abilities including: levitation, teleportation, transmutation, metamorphosis and the projection of thought-forms.

Psychosomatic is now becoming more widely accepted as what all illness is because of the inescapable evidence of the mind/body connection. Although the common use of the term meaning 'it's all in one's head' does not apply because the illness is not imaginary, it is in fact quite real.

Quantum (quanta - plural) is the most fundamental or the smallest unit or quantity of energy, light or photon.

Quantum Physics deals with the study of the behavior of quanta, specifically matter and energy at the molecular level. Max Planck is attributed to its inception.

Quantum Theory is the most important discovery in the scientific community of this century and describes the nature of the universe very differently than anything prior, especially, relativity.

Reincarnation is an accepted concept in many of the world's religions including Spiritism and New Age circles.

Sadhana is Sanskrit for spiritual exertion.

Samasti is Sanskrit for the highest level of the collective.

Sanskrit is one of the oldest Indo-European languages, dating back to 1200 b.c. It is still spoken in parts of India, but mostly is the language of literary and religious scholars.

Satori is the phenomenological state of higher consciousness, often called enlightenment. Zen Buddhists call it illumination or spiritual illumination, and achieve it through rigorous meditation practices.

Second wave/force, or the second major movement of psychology to appear is considered by most to be all the theories that focus on behavior. For the purpose of this analysis the Gestalt Therapies are placed in this category.

Self Evolution is the concept introduced by Carl Jung that posits a continuing incarnation of the individual's transcendental or higher Self through integration of the personality. This concept is being promoted by evolutionaries like Barbara Marx Hubbard who writes on her website, "Self-evolution, then, is the process of becoming a co-creator with the impulse of creation itself. The maturation of our species finds its expression in each of us unfolding the divine within."[1] This Self is seen as the essential aspect of our being that is directly animated by Source, by Spirit. It is the localized, individualized aspect of the Process of Creation, the God-force, and the Impulse of Evolution. This Self has been in the past often projected onto gods and ascended beings. Now, as the human species slowly matures, this Self is incarnating as our own essence, our own incarnation of spirit, our own individual expression of the divine.

Shamanic Healing is a method of healing with deep roots in indigenous populations dating back thousands of years. This form of healing is appropriate for illnesses or problems which have a spiritual cause. The shamanic practitioner works with the aid of his helping spirits, guides or power animals to bring healing

---

[1] www.barbaramarxhubbard.com

to the patient. Shamanic healing practices are conducted mostly via the shamanic journey. Techniques include extraction, power animal retrieval, soul retrieval, soul conduction, and divination. There has been a tremendous rise in interest in shamanic practices. It is becoming more understood that this is an indication that the species is evolving into a more spiritually-based Homo luminous, Homo universalis, or Homo angelicus species.

Shamanic Journey is literally a journey in consciousness with the intent of bridging the ordinary reality of everyday awareness with the non-ordinary or altered states of higher consciousness. Traditionally reserved for The Shaman of indigenous peoples, this practice is gaining popularity as a tool for individuals to help heal their own bodies, minds, spirits, and life's path or to help others.

Shift. See THE SHIFT

Spiritism is a philosophy made popular by Allan Kardec. It differs only slightly from Spiritualism because it is not a religion. It has no leader or churches, only centers.

Spirituality refers to all or any matters of spirit, or being spiritual. It usually refers to that part of the vital life force of the universe, the individual or reality itself, that is invisible, immaterial or intangible, but can be known by deliberate discovery through spiritual practices. Although Webster mentions religious connectivity to the term it is most commonly used with a decided distinction apart from religion. For instance, one might say "I'm spiritual, not religious," but would not bother to say (or perhaps not dare to admit) "I'm religious, not spiritual."

Spiritual practices most typically include meditation, prayer, contemplation, and some forms of divination. Spiritual practices less typically include induced trance states; usually through dance or drumming, induced or accidental out-of-body experiences, and the use of hallucinogens to experience altered states. This can include hypnosis and self-hypnosis, although these are not usually considered spiritual practices.

Spiritualism has been called a science, as well as, a philosophy and is considered a religion, by some. The most common practice within spiritualism is mediumship, or the act or ability to communicate with the dead. Spiritualism can be misunderstood for spirituality because in its broader sense they are inclusive. However, not all spiritually-minded individuals who use spiritually based practices are interested in or involved with spiritualism.

Spiritualist is an individual who may either be considered a medium or a channel.

String Theory states that there are molecular strings that vibrate at specific frequencies rather than particles as in quantum theory.

Subtle Energy is the vital/divine/spiritual force or life force found in all things in the entire universe.

Sufism is the mystical tradition of the Islamic religion. Practitioners are known as Sufis and belong to Sufi Orders. Practices are designed to produce the experience of God as ecstatic love. The most famous practice is Whirling Dervish dancing and the most famous Sufi poet is Rumi.

Super conscious telepathy is a term from parapsychology that involves accessing collective wisdom, such as the Akashic Records to obtain and provide knowledge.

Techlepathy is technologically enabled telepathy. It has become renowned with the popular computer toys and games like MindFlex by Mattel and NeuroSky, where the player moves objects by concentrating on them. Thus, brain-computer interfaces are not only capable of training individuals, but also of validating telepathy in the scientific community.

Telekinesis is a term derived from the Greek root for distance- tele and kinesis for motion- the movement of objects. The term is often mistakenly used interchangeably with psycho kinesis.

Telepathy is typically referred to as thought transference or mind reading. The word is derived from the Greek root for distance- tele and pathe for experience. The scientific community basically still denies its existence. The parapsychological community defines it as extra-sensory perception with definitions for latent, emotive and other types. (SEE LATENT TELEPATHY, INTUITIVE, EMOTIVE AND SUPER CONSCIOUS TELEPATHY DEFINITIONS)

The Great Shift or The Shift are terms that have gained momentum over the last decade to designate this time in history, as a time in which the consciousness (individual and collective) of the human species shifts, from being self-centered or ego-centric, to energy or divine centered and universally oriented. There is tremendous consensus among the scientific, astronomical, historical, philosophical, theosophical, archaeological, and indigenous communities, (as well as, visionaries and prophets) that this is in fact a real phenomenon. Unfortunately, The Shift has come to be almost synonymous with the end of the world, because so many of the predictions are centered around December 21, 2012. This date simply marked the end of the last recorded (5200 year cycle) ancient Mayan calendar. Contemporary Mayan elders insist this does not mean the end of the world (as doomsdayers predicted), but rather the end of the world as we know it, signifying a new beginning. (See definition of the New Humanity) Specifically, to differing cultural factions The Shift indicates things like: the Second Coming of Christ or the Christification of the Planet; the return of the Mayan god, Quetzalcoatl, the plumed serpent; the collapse of the third dimension- into the fourth and fifth dimensions where humans will dwell as gods; humanity's (only the righteous or the ready) Ascension into heaven; living in abundance and

Oneness with the Cosmos; deliverance into Utopia with help from friendly intergalactic races; and the disappearance of the modern-day Neanderthal man. (There is reportedly an eerie and astounding astrological and astronomical resemblance to the age when Neanderthal man went extinct). Generally, The Shift is considered a shift in the consciousness of man, an historical landmark of evolution when Homo sapiens wake up and realize that cooperation is imperative to the survival of our species, lest we destroy ourselves and our planet.

The New Human is a term that is growing in popularity as the concepts of Conscious Evolution and the Shift are becoming main-stream. It is generally agreed among futurists, philosophers, metaphysicians, scientists and the world's indigenous leaders (contemporary and ancient) that The New Human will consciously and deliberately activate increased strands (up to 12) of DNA. This activation process effects genetic, molecular and glandular changes, allowing higher frequencies of energetic or divine vibration to govern the individual's body, mind, and spirit. DNA activation connects the individual with his or her own energetic layers, as well as, universal layers of consciousness, especially the noosphere. The new human will have superior telekinetic and telepathic capabilities which will render miracles and serendipity commonplace. This ideology differs from Transhumanism because new human advances are made via consciousness, rather than technology.

The New Humanity of Homo sapiens (wise man) will be connected to each other and to the earth and the universe, telepathically, by the noosphere. Humans will be fully cooperative with each other and with energetic or divine principles, existing harmoniously with nature and the universe. Democratic and altruistic principles will govern all aspects of human endeavor. There is a growing body of speculation that Homo sapiens already exist as differing species. Frank White, author of The Overview Effect: Space Exploration and Human Evolution, (1998) told Barbara Marx Hubbard, in August of 2012 during a Maestro phone conference, he believes we should start out calling ourselves Homo egoicus (rather than Homo sapiens) because we are so entrenched with our egoic minds. He posits we can then begin to differentiate, for example by calling ourselves Homo transitionalis, while we collectively work toward becoming Homo holisticus or Homo luminous. White further believes a new genus is evolving. He is naming it Psyche Materialis (soul in the material) and believes that the individuals of this genus of mankind will have fully-functioning Christ-like, Homo-luminous light-bodies.

Third wave/force, or the third major movement of psychology is generally considered the Humanistic Therapies. However, in Celestial Psychology, the third wave consists of Interpersonal Therapies and the Cognitive Therapies, while the Humanistic therapies are included with the Transpersonal therapies of the fourth wave.

Thought forms are created when strong positive or negative thoughts become imprinted on the etheric layer or noosphere.

Transactional Analysis (TA) is a systematic categorization of the games the ego plays, with the goal of improving QOL. It was created by Eric Berne, MD, in the late fifties, and gained world recognition with his book, Games People Play (1964). It remains a viable theoretical system for consciousness-raising within the Interpersonal Psychotherapies.

Transformation in metaphysical terms includes any complete change in matter or energy. The alchemists believed they could transform lead into gold. Although this was mostly considered allegory for transforming the lead of a dense personality into the gold of higher consciousness.

Transhumanism is a movement to transcend the human condition with technological advances like cryonics and robotics.

Transpersonal Psychology was founded in the early 1970s by Abraham Maslow, Anthony Sutich, Roberto Assagilio, and later Stanislov Grof after they realized that Humanistic Psychology (all were involved but Grof in founding Humanistic) was missing a spiritual component, which they sought to incorporate into Transpersonal theoretical approaches.

Woo-woo or woo is a term used to connote that which is of the occult, mysterious, or not rational and of the New Age. Skeptics may use it in a derogatory way meaning nonsense or quackery.

Work, the or Work, is a term brought forth by George Ivanovitch Gurdjieff (c. 1866-1949) in the early 1900s. He spent many years as a student of various mystery schools in the East, and is still considered today, by many to be the founding father of Western contemporary non-traditional spirituality. The term is based on the teaching that man is asleep to his true nature, therefore, in order to "wake-up" one must utilize self-remembering techniques. These techniques have been organized under the broader umbrella of The Fourth Way by his students who have kept his Work alive, by writing books and maintaining schools all over the world. Today, The Work includes any consciousness-raising activities or any Work on oneself, that is designed to not only wake up the individual, but also improve their QOl, as in psychotherapy. Contemporary author Byron Katie appears to have claimed the phrase as her own, with no easily found- if available at all- attestation to its origin.

Zero Point is an altered state of consciousness, sometimes identified as Alpha level, where one is still alert, yet also aware of the nothingness. This state is usually attained with meditation and/or hypnosis.

Zero Point Energy (ZPE) Field and Zero Fluctuations Field (ZPF) are terms in quantum physics being developed by physicists, and scientists that began as far back as Einstein around 1913. Originally, it was thought a vacuum existed in between sub-atomic particles in every cell. Now, they recognize there are particles in the vacuum, and they fluctuate and create energy from seeming nothingness or the "zero point." Hence, the name ZPE.

Notes

Chapter 1

1. 15

Chapter 2

2. *Eastern Body, Western Mind: Psychology and the Chakra System as a Path to the Self*, Judith, A. 2004. *Celestial Arts Berkeley, 8*.

3. http://www.coreevolution.com/john_pierrakos.php

4. Ibid.

5. Ibid.

6. http://www.barbarabrennan.com/aboutbarbara/about_barbara.html

7. *Eastern Body, Western Mind: Psychology and the Chakra System as a Path to the Self*, Judith, A. 2004. *Celestial Arts Berkeley, xii.*

Chapter 3

8. Most modern-day practitioners use politically correct terms of client or consumer rather than patient.

9. *Systems of Psycholtherapy: A Transtheoretical Analysis*, Prochaska and Norcross, Books/Cole Publishers, *1994, 460.*

Chapter 4

10. *Systems of Psychotherapy: A Transtheoretical Analysis*, Prochaska and Norcross, Brooks/Cole Publishers, *1994, 93-95.*

11. *Existential Psychotherapy*, Irvin D. Yalom, Basic Books, 1990, 8-9.

12. *See the work of Mike Dooley and the book The Secret for more information.*

13. *Existential Psychotherapy, Irvin D. Yalom, Basic Books, 1990, 8-9.*

14. *Systems of Psychotherapy: A Transtheoretical Analysis, Prochaska and Norcross, Brooks/Cole Publishers, 1994, 101.*

15. Ibid.

16. *Existential Psychotherapy, Irvin D. Yalom, Basic Books, 1990, 245.*

Chapter 5

17. Paramahansa Yogananda (1893–1952), regarded as the father of Yoga, is credited with introducing meditation to the Western world. http://www.yogananda-srf.org

18. *Systems of Psychotherapy: A Transtheoretical Analysis, Prochaska and Norcross, Brooks/Cole Publishers, 1994, 164-165.*

Chapter 6

19. *Systems of Psychotherapy: A Transtheoretical Analysis, Prochaska and Norcross, Brooks/Cole Publishers, 1994, 201.*

Chapter 7

20. *Systems of Psychotherapy: A Transtheoretical Analysis, Prochaska and Norcross, Brooks/Cole Publishers, 1994, 320.*

21. *Systems of Psychotherapy: A Transtheoretical Analysis, Prochaska and Norcross, Brooks/Cole Publishers, 1994, 331.*

22. Likert scales (named after Rensis Likert, Ph.D (1903–1981)) are usually 4 or 5 point multiple choice quizzes designed to provide data for analysis, usually as an evaluation or survey.

Chapter 8

23. *Religions, Values, and Peak-Experiences, Abraham H. Maslow. Penguin Books, New York, NY 1976, 59-62.*

24. *The concept of the egoic mind is becoming mainstream through the work of authors like Eckhart Tolle and the teachings of large bodies of work like A Course in Miracles. SEE GLOSSARY.*

25. *Systems of Psychotherapy: A Transtheoretical Analysis, Prochaska and Norcross, Brooks/Cole Publishers, 1994, 62-66.*

26. *Religions, Values, and Peak-Experiences, Abraham H. Maslow, Penguin Books, New York, NY, 1976, 11.*

27. *When the Impossible Happens: Adventures in Non-Ordinary Realities, Stanislav Grof, M.D., Ph.D. Sounds True, Inc. 2006, xvi.*

Chapter 9

28. 26.

29. Evolutionary Enlightenment: A New Path to Spiritual Awakening, Andrew Cohen, 2012, 25

30. Ibid., 27.

31. Ibid., 93.

32. *EnlightenNext magazine, October–December, 2004 In Memoriam*

33. *The Evolutionary Journey: A Personal Guide to a Positive Future. Barbara Marx Hubbard. Evolutionary Press, San Francisco, CA., back cover.*

34. *Appendix/Handout from workshop (6/1/09) for Twelve Foundations of Unitive Psychology, 1.*

Chapter 10

35. *Navigating the Collapse of Time, Cowan, 112.*

Bibliography & Recommended Reading

A Course in Miracles. Tiburon, CA: Foundation for Inner Peace, 1975.

Argüelles, Jose'. Manifesto for the Noosphere: *The Next Stage in the Evolution of Human Consciouness.* Berkley: Evolver Press, 2011.

Bauman, Peter & Taft, Michael W. *Ego: The Fall of the Twin Towers and the Rise of an Enlightened Humanity.* San Francisco: NE Press, 2011.

Blackburn Losey, Meg. *The Secret History of Consciousness.* San Francisco: Weiser Books, 2010.

Blackburn Losey, Meg. *Touching the Light- What Miracles Are Made Of.* San Francisco: Weiser Books, 2011.

Braden, Gregg. *The Divine Matrix: Bridging Time, Space, Miracles and Belief.* Carlsbad, CA: Hay House, 2007.

Braschler, Von. *7 Secrets of Time Travel: Mystic Voyages of the Energy Body.* Rochester, VT: Destiny Books, 2012.

Brennan, Barbara Ann. *Hands of Light: A Guide to Healing Through the Human Energy Field.* New York: Bantam, 1987.

Brussat, Frederic & Mary Ann. *Spiritual Literacy- Reading the Sacred in Everyday Life.* New York: Scribner, 1996.

Byrne, Rhonda. *The Secret.* New York: Beyond Words Publishing, 2006.

Chernin, Dennis, K. *How to Meditate Using Chakras, Mantra, and Breath*. Ann Arbor: Think Publishing, 2006.

Chopra, Deepak. *The Seven Spiritual Laws of Success*. San Rafael, CA: Amber-Allen Publishing, 1994.

de Chardin, Teilhard. *The Divine Milieu*. New York: Harper & Row, 1960.

de Chardin, Teilhard. *The Future of Man*. New York: Harper & Row, 1964.

Cohen, Andrew. *Evolutionary Enlightenment: A New Path to Spiritual Awakening*. New York: Select Books, 2011.

Dyer, Wayne. *There is a Spiritual Solution to Every Problem*. Quill Publishers: New York, 2003.

Feinstein, David. *Energy Psychology Interactive— Rapid Interventions for Lasting Change*. Ashland, OR: Innersource, 2004.

Gallo, Fred & Vincenzi, Harry. *Energy Tapping*. Oakland, CA: New Harbinger Publications, 2008.

Goldberg, Bruce. *Self Hypnosis - Easy Ways to Hypnotize Your Problems Away*. Franklin Lakes, NJ: The Career Press, 2006.

Goswami, Amit. *The Self Aware Universe– How Consciousness creates the Material World*. New York: Penguin Putnam, 1993.

Grayson, Henry. *Use Your Body to Heal Your Mind: Revolutionary Methods to Release All Barriers to Health, Healing and Happiness*. Bloomington, IN: Balboa Press, 2012.

Green, Martin. *Prophets of a New Age- Counterculture and the Politics of Hope*. Mount Jackson, VA: Axios Press, 1992.

Gregg, Susan. *The Complete Idiot's Guide to Spiritual Healing*. Indianapolis: Macmillan USA, 2000.

Grof, Stanislav. *When the Impossible Happens– Adventures in Non-Ordinary Realities*. Boulder: Sounds True, 2006.

Hall, Judy. *The Encyclopedia of Crystals*. Beverly, MA: Quayside Publishing Group, 2006.

Harris, Bill. *Managing Evolutionary Growth– How to Create Deep Change Without Falling Apart*. Beaverton, OR: Centerpointe Research Institute, 1990.

Harris, Bill. *Thresholds of the Mind*. Beaverton, OR: Centerpointe Research Institute, 2007.

Hubbard, Barbara Marx. *Birth 2012 and Beyond: Humanity's Great Shift to the Age of Conscious Evolution*. Shift Books, 2012.

Hubbard, Barbara Marx. *Conscious Evolution: Awakening the Power of Our Social Potential*. Novato, CA: New World Library, 1998.

Hubbard, Barbara Marx. *Emergence- The Shift from Ego to Essence- Ten Steps to the Universal Human*. Charlottesville, VA: Hampton Roads Publishing, 2001.

Hubbard, Barbara Marx. *The Evolutionary Journey: A Personal Guide To A Positive Future-* San Francisco, Evolutionary Press, 1982.

Hubbard, Barbara Marx. *52 Codes for Conscious Evolution: A Process of Metamorphosis to Realize Our Full Potential Self.* Santa Barbara, CA: Foundation for Conscious Evolution, 2011.

Hurtak, J.J. *The Book of Knowledge-The Keys of Enoch.* Los Gatos, CA: The Academy for Future Science. 1977.

Jampolsky, Lee. *Healing the Addictive Mind: Freeing yourself from Addictive Patterns and Relationships.* New York: Celestial Arts, 1991.

Judith, Anodea. *Ckakra Balancing— A Guide to Healing and Awakening your Energy Body.* Boulder: Sounds True Publishing, 2003.

Judith, Anodea. *Eastern Body, Western Mind: Psychology and the Chakra System as a Path to the Self.* Berkeley: Celestial Arts, 1996.

Kabat-Zinn, John. *Wherever You Go There You Are— Mindfulness Meditation in Everyday Life.* New York: Hyperion, 1994.

Keyes, Ken, Jr. *Handbook to Higher Consciousness.* Marina del Rey, CA: Living Love Publications, 1975.

La Cerra, Peggy. & Bingham, Roger. *The Origin of Minds— Evolution, Uniqueness, and the New Science of the Self.* New York: Harmony Books, 2002.

Lesser, Elizabeth. *The Seeker's Guide: Making Your Life A Spiritual Adventure.* New York: Villard Publishing, 1999.

Lipton, Bruce. *The Biology of Belief.* Carlsbad, CA: Hay House, 2005.

Maslow, Abraham. *Religions, Values, and Peak-Experiences.* NY. Penguin Books, 1976.

McTaggart, Lynne. *The Field: The Quest for the Secret Force of the Universe.* New York: Harper Collins Publishers, 2008.

Myss, Caroline. *Anatomy of the Spirit: The Seven Stages of Power and Healing,* New York: Three Rivers Press, 1996.

Pearl, Eric. *The Reconnection -Heal Others, Heal Yourself.* Carlsbad, CA: Hay House, 2001.

Phipps, Carter. *Evolutionaries: Unlocking the Spiritual and Cultural Potential of Science's Greatest Idea.* New York: Harper Perennial, 2012.

Pierrakos, Eva. *The Pathwork of Self-Transformation.* New York, Bantam Books, 1990.

Pierrakos, John. *Core Energetics: Developing the Capacity to Love and Heal.* Mendocino, CA: Liferhythms, 1990.

Prochaska, James & Norcross, John. *Systems of Psychotherapy-A Transtheoretical Analysis.* Pacific Grove, CA: Brooks/Cole Publishing 1994.

Rich, Mark. *Energetic Anatomy: An Illustrated Guide to Understand and Using the Human Energy System.* Dallas: Life Align, 2004.

Sherwood, Keith. *Chakra Healing and Karmic Awareness*. St. Paul, MN: Llewellyn
  Publications, 2005.

Sperry, Len. *Spirituality in Clinical Practice: Theory and Practice of Spiritually Oriented
  Psychotherapy*. New York: Routledge Taylor & Francis Group, 2011.

Tolle, Eckhart. *A New Earth– Awakening to Your Life's Purpose*. New York: Plume
  Publishing, 2005.

Vennells, David F. *Reiki for Beginners- Mastering Natural Healing Techniques*. St. Paul,
  MN: Llewellyn Publishing, 2002.

Wauters, Ambika. *The Book of Chakras: Discover the Hidden Forces Within You*.
  Happauge, NY: Barron's Educational Series, .2002.

Welwood, John. *Toward a Psychology of Awakening–Buddhism, Psychotherapy, and the path of
  Personal and Spiritual Transformation*. Boston: Shambhala Publications, 2000.

Wilber, Ken. *Integral Psychology*. Boston: Shambala Publications, 2000.

Wilber, Ken. *Integral Spirituality*. Boston: Integral Books, 2007.

Wilber, Ken. *The Spectrum of Consciousness*. Wheaton, IL: Theosophical Publishing
  House, 1977.

ABOUT THE AUTHOR

Celeste Emelia Mattingly, LCSW is a graduate of the MSW Advanced Generalist Program at Springfield College, in Springfield, MA. She has over 28 years experience working in a variety of recovery settings. She founded Psychotherapy Healing Services, LLC in 1999 and has maintained a successful private practice serving hundreds of adults with mental health and addiction issues. In 2008 she branded her own eclectic theory of psychotherapy, suitably named Celestial Psychology®. CP is a skillful blend of standard psychiatric techniques and state-of-the art holistic practices including The Reconnection® healing modality.

Celeste began her metaphysical studies in the 1970s, with the teachings of Krishnamurti, Gurdjeiff, Ouspensky, Wilber and others. She completed a 40-Day Arica training in Amherst, MA in 1973, with Oscar Ichazo of Arica, Chile. Her studies included: Silva Mind Control; Unity; A Course in Miracles; Twelve-Steps; and a wide variety of world's religions. In 2002 she completed the Reiki Level I & II training in the USUI tradition, and became a Universal Life Church Reverend. Celeste is an authorized facilitator of The Reconnection healing method. She is a graduate of Barbara Marx Hubbard's Ego to Essence and the Agent of Conscious Evolution (ACE) training. Currently, she is studying alternative healing methods with Gene Ang, Ph.D. of California.

In 2009 Celeste founded The Center for Holistic Empowerment, located in Bloomfield, CT. The Center hosts a variety of events to bring spirituality to the community. A year later, she founded Celeste Emelia's School of Consciousness-Raising (CESCR). CESCR is the culmination of a 40-year dream. After Celeste completed the 40-Day Arica Training in the 1970s, her mother dreamt of her deceased mother Emelia whom Celeste is named after. Grandmother Emelia was shaking her finger and emphatically stating, "Celeste should start a school. Celeste should start a consciousness-raising school!" Hence, the school's name. At CESCR Celeste holds National Association of Social Workers (NASW) approved Spirituality workshops for Social Workers, Marriage and Family Therapist, and Counselors to receive their Continuing Education Credits. She also provides ongoing spiritual empowerment classes for professionals and laypersons.

Celeste's healing and teaching methods help clients, students, and workshop participants to master emotions, overcome addictions, and negative behavior; as well as, improve coping, communication, stress and anger management skills. Her work encourages all to access their own strengths, innate healing abilities and raise their consciousness - naturally- to promote profound and permanent change.

celestemattinglylcsw.com
celestialpsychology.com

ABOUT THE EDITOR

Linda Moore works with those who are inspired to communicate with words and want a collaborator to help with some or all phases of the project including development, writing, rewriting, or editing. Over the past twenty years, she has had the pleasure of helping talented professionals articulate and present information they wish to share with readers. Linda received a bachelor's degree in sociology from Allegheny College in 1977. She was employed for several decades as an Executive Assistant to level-one executives, routinely serving as the office copy editor and proofreader. Linda employs her knowledge stockpile with every project. She has completed grammar, writing, and editing coursework, and she routinely participates in professional development opportunities for editors. She is a published ghostwriter.

Linda lives in Cambridge, New York, surrounded by four generations of beloved family members. When she is not visiting her daughter in Colorado or listening to the ocean from a lesser-known beach, she is likely at her computer poring over dictionary-, grammar-, thesaurus-, or copy editing-related blogs and websites. A motley herd of four-legged friends, former rescue shelter residents, keep her company while she fusses over manuscript minutia.

In the words of Mark Twain:
"Say what [you propose] to say, not merely come near it.
Use the right word, not its second cousin.
Eschew surplusage.
[Do] not omit necessary details.
Avoid slovenliness of form.
Use good grammar.
Employ a simple and straightforward style."

Indeed.

Celestial ✹ Psychology®

Celestial Psychology® - Reconnecting Where Mind & Body Meet Spirit, is an eclectic blend of Standard Psychiatric Techniques and state-of-the-art holistic modalities. Celestial Psychology® is founded on the belief that human beings are capable of change, and that the most profound vehicle for change is consciousness-raising.

Celestial Psychology® Enterprises

The mission of CP Enterprises is to promote the evolution of the individual and of mankind by utilizing the consciousness-raising principles of Celestial Psychology. These principles focus on the integration of the body, mind and spirit, thereby ensuring good mental, physical, emotional, and spiritual health, for generations to come.

Visit our website celestialpsychology.com to download a free "7 Days to Your Luminous Self" e-book. Visit our online store to order your stunning CP mandala-art plate or other promotional products, mugs, tees, tanks and tote bags. 10% of the proceeds from these products will be divided among United Way, National Alliance for the Mentally Ill (NAMI) and Connecticut Community for Addictions Recovery (CCAR).

Angel investors and book publishers contact: cmattingly100@comcast.net

17775268R00112

Made in the USA
Charleston, SC
28 February 2013